P9-APP-961

VICTORIAN POETS

VICTORIAN POETS

By <u>AMY SHARP</u>

> 'I give you the end of a golden string,
> Only wind it into a ball;
> It will lead you in at Heaven's gate,
> Built in Jerusalem's wall.'
>
> BLAKE.

KENNIKAT PRESS
Port Washington, N. Y./London

VICTORIAN POETS

First published in 1891
Reissued in 1970 by Kennikat Press
Library of Congress Catalog Card No: 70-105834
ISBN 0-8046-1053-3

Manufactured by Taylor Publishing Company   Dallas, Texas

CONTENTS.

		PAGE
	LIST OF BOOKS	vii
	RECORD OF DATES	x
	INTRODUCTION	xvii
I.	ALFRED TENNYSON	I
II.	ROBERT BROWNING	40
III.	ELIZABETH BARRETT BROWNING	103
IV.	ARTHUR HUGH CLOUGH AND MATTHEW ARNOLD	121
V.	DANTE GABRIEL ROSSETTI, WILLIAM MORRIS, AND ALGERNON CHARLES SWINBURNE ...	157
VI.	MINOR POETS	186
	INDEX	205

CONTENTS

BOOKS.

[The most valuable books are marked with two asterisks; those marked with one asterisk come next in importance.]

I. POETS' WORKS.

Tennyson. 'Works,' 7 vols., Macmillan, 5*s.* each.
    **'Works,' 1 vol. (complete to year 1880), 7*s.* 6*d.*

R. Browning. 'Works,' 16 vols., Smith & Elder, 5*s.* each.
    (*Pippa Passes*, vol. iii., * *Colombe's Birthday*, vol. iv.,
    * *The Ring and the Book*, vols. viii.—x.)
    **'Selections,' 2 vols., 3*s.* 6*d.* each.
    'Selections,' 1 vol., 1*s.*

E. B. Browning. 'Works,' 6 vols., Smith & Elder, 5*s.* each.
    **'Selections,' 2 vols., 3*s.* 6*d.* each.
    *'Aurora Leigh,' 7*s.* 6*d.*

A. H. Clough. **'Poems,' Macmillan, 7*s.* 6*d.*

M. Arnold. 'Poems,' 3 vols., Macmillan, 7*s.* 6*d.* each.
    **'Complete Poetical Works,' 1 vol., 7*s.* 6*d.*
    *'Selections,' 4*s.* 6*d.*

D. G. Rossetti. **'Works,' 2 vols., Ellis & Elvey, 18*s.*

W. Morris. *'Defence of Guenevere, and Other Poems,'
    Reeves & Turner, 8*s.*
    **'The Earthly Paradise,' 10 parts, 3*s.* 6*d.* each, or
    1 vol., 7*s.* 6*d.*
    *'Story of Sigurd the Volsung,' 6*s.*

A. C. Swinburne. **'Selections,' Chatto & Windus, 6*s.*
    *'Atalanta in Calydon,' 6*s.*
    *'Songs before Sunrise,' 10*s.* 6*d.*

II. Books of Criticism and Reference.

'The most valuable critic is the critic who communicates sympathy by an exquisite record of his own delights.'—E. DOWDEN.

(A) GENERAL.

Abbott and Seeley. *English Lessons for English People* (chapters on the Diction of Poetry and Metre), Seeley, Jackson & Halliday, 4s. 6d.

M. Arnold. *Essays in Criticism*, 2nd Series (The Study of Poetry), Macmillan, 7s. 6d.

E. C. Stedman. *Victorian Poets*, Chatto & Windus, 9s.

H. Buxton Forman. *Our Living Poets.*

R. H. Hutton. *Literary Essays* (Tennyson, Browning, Clough, Arnold), Macmillan, 5s.

E. Dowden. *Transcripts and Studies* (Victorian Literature); *Studies in Literature* (Tennyson, Browning).

A. C. Swinburne. *Essays and Studies* (Rossetti, Morris, Arnold), Chatto & Windus, 12s.

T. H. Ward. *The English Poets*, vol. iv., Macmillan, 7s. 6d.

(B) SPECIAL.

For Tennyson. *Lord Tennyson: A Biographical Sketch*, by H. J. Jennings. Chatto & Windus, 6s.

Tennysoniana, R. H. Shepherd.

The Poetry of Tennyson, H. Van Dyke.

A Key to Tennyson's 'In Memoriam,' A. Gatty, 3s. 6d. ;

or,

An Analysis of 'In Memoriam,' F. W. Robertson. Kegan Paul, 2s. (also reprinted in Robertson's 'Lectures, Addresses, and Literary Remains,' 5s.)

Studies in Tennyson's Idylls, H. Elsdale. Kegan Paul, 5s.

Taine's *History of English Literature* (English Trans.), BOOK v., ch. iii. Chatto & Windus, 15s.

Notes to Selected Lyrics, by F. T. Palgrave. Macmillan, 4s. 6d.

For R. Browning. *Bibliography*, F. J. Furnivall. Trübner & Co.

* *A Handbook to the Works of R. Browning*, Mrs. Sutherland Orr. George Bell, 6*s*.

An Introduction to the Study of Browning, A. Symons, 2*s*. 6*d*.

Essays on R. Browning's Poetry, J. T. Nettleship, 7*s*. 6*d*.

Studies in the Poetry of R. Browning, J. Fotheringham, 6*s*.

Essay on Browning in *Obita Dicta*, 1st Series, A. Birrell.

For E. B. Browning. *Elizabeth Barrett Browning*, J. H. Ingram (Eminent Women Series).

For A. H. Clough. *Literary Studies*, vol. ii., Bagehot.

For D. G. Rossetti. *Dante Gabriel Rossetti*, W. M. Rossetti, 7*s*. 6*d*.

Dante Gabriel Rossetti, J. Knight (Great Writers Series), 1*s*.

Recollections of D. G. Rossetti, T. Hall Caine.

* Article in *Encyl. Brit.*, by Theodore Watts.

For Sonnet Structure. *Milton's Sonnets*, edited with Introduction and Notes by Mark Pattison. Kegan Paul, 6*s*.

III. SOME MINOR POETRY.

Emily Brontë. 'Poems by Ellis Bell,' appended to 'The Professor,' Smith & Elder, 2*s*. 6*d*.

Jean Ingelow. 'Poems,' 2 vols., Longmans, 12*s*.

Christina Rossetti. 'Poems,' Macmillan, 7*s*. 6*d*.

Mrs. Hamilton King. 'The Disciples,' Kegan Paul, 6*s*.

George Eliot. 'The Spanish Gypsy,' 'The Legend of Jubal, and Other Poems,' Macmillan, each 5*s*.

William Barnes. 'Poems of Rural Life in the Dorset Dialect,' Kegan Paul, 8*s*.

'Fo'c'sl' Yarns,' Macmillan, 7*s*. 6*d*.

Austin Dobson. 'Old World Idylls,' 'At the Sign of the Lyre,' Kegan Paul, each 6*s*.

C. S. Calverly. 'Fly Leaves,' Deighton, Bell & Co., 3*s*. 6*d*.

W. G. Courthope. 'The Paradise of Birds,' Hatchards, 7*s*. 6*d*.

Lewis Morris. 'Collected Poems,' 1 vol., 6*s*.

Sir Edwin Arnold. 'The Light of Asia' (Lotus Series), 3*s*. 6*d*.

Charles Kingsley. 'Poems,' Macmillan, 1*s*. 6*d*.

James Thomson. 'The City of Dreadful Night,' 5*s*.

Cardinal Newman. 'Verses on Various Occasions,' 3*s*. 6*d*.

F. W. H. Myers. 'St. Paul,' Macmillan, 2*s*. 6*d*.

RECORD OF DATES.

ALFRED TENNYSON.

'In poetry illustrious and consummate ; in friendship noble and sincere.'
R. BROWNING.

1809. Born Aug. 5 at Somersby in Lincolnshire.

1827. Publication of ' Poems by Two Brothers.'

1828. Matriculation at Trinity College, Cambridge.

1829. Prize poem on 'Timbuctoo.'

1830. ' Poems, chiefly Lyrical.'

> [*Claribel, Lilian, The Owl, The Merman, Ode to Memory, Mariana, Recollections of the Arabian Nights*, etc.]

1832. ' Poems.'

> [*The Lady of Shalott, Eleänore, Margaret, The Miller's Daughter, The Palace of Art, The May Queen, Fatima, The Lotos-Eaters, A Dream of Fair Women*, etc.]

1833. ' The Lover's Tale.'

,,   Death of 'A. H. H.'—Arthur Henry Hallam, son of the historian, born Feb. 1, 1811, was educated at Eton and Trinity College, Cambridge, graduated in 1832, died suddenly at Vienna on Sept. 15. His body was brought back to England by sea and buried in Clevedon Church, Somersetshire, Jan. 3, 1834.

1842. ' Poems,' 2 vols.

> [*Morte d'Arthur, The Gardener's Daughter, Dora, Godiva, Locksley Hall, The Day Dream, St. Simeon Stylites, Ulysses, Tithonus, The Lord of Burleigh, Sir Galahad, The Vision of Sin*, and others.]

1847. 'The Princess.'
1850. 'In Memoriam.'
   ,,   Appointed Poet-Laureate in succession to Wordsworth.
   ,,   Marriage.
1852. Death of the Duke of Wellington.
1854. Battle of Balaclava : 'Charge of the Light Brigade.'
1855. 'Maud, and Other Poems.'
1859. 'Idylls of the King.'
       [*Enid, Elaine, Vivien, Guinevere.*]
1861. Death of the Prince Consort.
1864. 'Enoch Arden, and Other Poems.'
1869. 'Idylls of the King.'
       [*The Holy Grail, Pelleas and Ettarre, Coming of Arthur, Passing of Arthur.*]
1872. 'Idylls of the King.'
       [*Gareth and Lynette, The Last Tournament.*]
1875. 'Queen Mary.'
1877. 'Harold.'
1880. 'Ballads and Other Poems.'
1884. Raised to the Peerage, as Baron Tennyson of Aldworth, Surrey, and Farringdon, Freshwater, Isle of Wight, Jan. 24.
   ,,   'The Cup.'
   ,,   'Becket.'
   ,,   'Tiresias, and Other Poems.'
1886. Death of Lord Tennyson's younger son.
   ,,   'Locksley Hall Sixty Years After, and Other Poems.'
1889. 'Demeter, and Other Poems.'

ROBERT BROWNING, 1812—1889.

1812. Born at Camberwell, near London.
1833. Publication of 'Pauline.'
1835. 'Paracelsus.'
1837. 'Strafford.'
1840. 'Sordello.'

1841. 'Bells and Pomegranates.'   1. 'Pippa Passes.'
1842.   „   „   2. 'King Victor and King
                                        Charles.'

 „   „   „   3. 'Dramatic Lyrics.'
1843.   „   „   4. 'The Return of the
                                        Druses.'

 „   „   „   5. 'A Blot in the 'Scut-
                                        cheon.'

1844.   „   „   6. 'Colombe's Birthday.'
1845.   „   „   7. 'Dramatic Romances
                                        and Lyrics.'

1846.   „   „   8. 'Luria,' 'A Soul's
                                        Tragedy.'

 „   Marriage to Miss Elizabeth Barrett.
1849. 'Poems,' 2 vols.
1850. 'Christmas Eve and Easter Day.'
1855. 'Men and Women.'
        [Fifty poems distributed in later editions under
        various titles.]
1861. Death of Mrs. Browning at Florence, June 29.
1864. 'Dramatis Personæ.'
1868. 'Collected Poetical Works.'
 „   'The Ring and the Book,' vols. i. ii.
1869.   „   „   „   vols. iii. iv.
1871. 'Balaustion's Adventure.'
 „   'Prince Hohenstiel-Schwangau, Saviour of Society.'
        [The Emperor Napoleon III. of France, 'in whom
        the cad, the coward, the idealist, and the sensualist
        were inextricably mixed.'—*Obita Dicta*.]
1872. 'Fifine at the Fair.'
        ['There is no harder reading.'—E. C. STEDMAN.]
1873. 'Red Cotton Nightcap Country ; or Turf and Towers.'
1875. 'Aristophanes' Apology' ; 'The Inn Album.'
1876. 'Pacchiarotto, and how he worked in Distemper.'
1877. 'The Agamemnon of Æschylus.'
1878. 'La Sairiaz' ; 'The Two Poets of Croisic.'
1879. 'Dramatic Idylls,' 1st Series.
1880.   „   „   2nd Series.

1880. Honorary degree of LL.D. conferred at Cambridge.
1882. Honorary degree of D.C.L. conferred at Oxford.
1883. 'Jocoseria.'
1884. 'Ferishtah's Fancies.'
1887. 'Parleyings with Certain People of Importance in their Day.'

> [Of many of these later poems it has been said they must 'have been written solely for the behoof of "The Browning Society," and not for mankind in general.'—R. H. HUTTON. The 'Dramatic Idylls' may be excepted.]

1889. 'Asolando.'
  ,,   Died at Venice.
  ,,   Buried in Westminster Abbey, Dec. 31.

ELIZABETH BARRETT BROWNING. 1809—1861.

1809. Probable date of birth.
1826. 'An Essay on Mind, and Other Poems' (anonymous, and not reprinted in collected works).
1832. 'Prometheus Bound, and Miscellaneous Poems.'
1838. 'The Seraphim, and Other Poems.'
1839. 'The Romaunt of the Page.'
1844. 'Poems,' 2 vols. (including 'A Drama of Exile').
1846. Marriage to Robert Browning.
1849. Birth of their son.
1850. 'Sonnets from the Portuguese.'
  ,,   'Poems,' 2nd edition.
1851. 'Casa Guidi Windows.'
1856. 'Aurora Leigh.'
1860. 'Poems before Congress.'
1861. Death at Florence, June 29.
1862. 'Last Poems.'

ARTHUR HUGH CLOUGH. 1819—1861.

'We have a foreboding that Clough, imperfect as he was in many respects, and dying before he had subdued his sensitive temperament to the sterner requirements of his art, will be thought a hundred years hence to have been the truest expression in verse of the moral and intellectual tendencies, the doubt and struggle towards settled convictions, of the period in which he lived.'—J. R. LOWELL, *My Study Windows*.

1819. Born at Liverpool, Jan. 1.
1829. Entered at Rugby School.
1837. Entered at Balliol College, Oxford.
1842. Elected Fellow of Oriel College.
1848. Resignation of Fellowship from religious scruples.
　　,,　　'Bothie of Tober-na-Vuolich.'
1849. 'Ambarvalia' (collection of poems).
　　,,　　Appointed Principal of University Hall, London.
　　,,　　'Amours de Voyage.' ⎫ (Written, but not published till
1850. 'Dipsychus.'　　　　　　⎭　　　some years later.)
1852. Removal to America.
1853. Appointed Examiner in the Education Office, Whitehall.
1854. Marriage.
1861. Death at Florence, Nov. 13.

MATTHEW ARNOLD. 1822—1888.

1822. Born at Laleham.
1845. Elected Fellow of Oriel College, Oxford.
1849. 'The Strayed Reveller, and Other Poems,' by 'A.'
1851. Marriage.
　　,,　　Appointed H.M. Inspector of Schools.
1852. 'Empedocles on Etna, and Other Poems.'
1853. 'Poems.'
1857. Elected Professor of Poetry at Oxford.
1858. 'Merope.'

1862. Re-elected Professor of Poetry at Oxford.
1876. Collected Poems, 2 vols.
1888. Death in April.

DANTE GABRIEL ROSSETTI. 1828—1882.

1828. Born in London, May 12.
1843. 'Sir Hugh the Heron' privately printed.
 „   Student in Cary's Art Academy.
1846. Student at Royal Academy.
1848. Works in studio of Ford Madox Brown.
 „   Establishment of Pre-Raphaelite Brotherhood.
1850. First number of 'The Germ,' Jan. 1.
1853. 'Sister Helen' in *Dusseldorf Annual*.
1860. Marriage at Hastings to Miss Eleanor Siddall, May 23.
1861. 'The Early Italian Poets.'
1862. Death of Mrs. D. G. Rossetti.
1870. 'Poems.'
1871. Controversy with Robert Buchanan.
1881. 'Ballads and Sonnets.'
1882. Death at Birchington-on-Sea, Easter Day (April 9).

WILLIAM MORRIS.

1834. Born.
1858. 'The Defence of Guenevere, and Other Poems' (dedi-
        cated to Rossetti).
1865. 'The Life and Death of Jason.'
1868-70. 'The Earthly Paradise.'
1869. 'The Story of Grettir the Strong' (translated from the
        Icelandic by E. Magnússon and W. Morris).
1872. 'Love is Enough.'
1875. 'The Æneids of Virgil done into English Verse.'
1876. 'The Story of Sigurd the Volsung.'

xvi   RECORD OF DATES.

1887. 'The Odyssey of Homer done into English Verse.'
1889. 'A Tale of the House of the Wolfings and all the
      Kindreds of the Mark' (written partly in prose).

ALGERNON CHARLES SWINBURNE.

1837. Born.
1861. 'The Queen Mother and Rosamond' (dedicated to
      Rossetti).
1864. 'Atalanta in Calydon.'
1865. 'Chastelard' (1st drama of Mary Stuart Trilogy).
1866. 'Poems and Ballads,' 1st Series.
  „   'Notes on Poems and Reviews.'
1867. 'A Song of Italy.'
1870. 'Ode on the French Republic.'
1871. 'Songs before Sunrise.'
1872. 'Under the Microscope.'
1874. 'Bothwell' (2nd drama in Mary Stuart Trilogy).
1876. 'Erechtheus' (2nd drama after Greek model).
1878. 'Poems and Ballads,' 2nd Series.
1880. 'Studies in Song'; 'Songs of the Springtides.'
1881. 'Mary Stuart' (3rd and concluding drama of the
      Trilogy).
1882. 'Tristram of Lyonesse, and Other Poems.'
1883. 'A Century of Roundels.'
1884. 'A Midsummer Holiday.'
1885. 'Marino Faliero' (drama).
1887. 'Locrine' (drama).
1889. 'Poems and Ballads,' 3rd Series.

INTRODUCTION.

CHARLES LAMB'S delicate humour finds, as usual, an exquisitely quaint and graceful expression for a feeling that many of us must have shared with him, when he says that he wants a form of grace before Poetry,—'a grace before Milton—a grace before Shakespeare—a devotional exercise proper to be said before reading the *Faërie Queene*.' Without the formalism of a form, he distils the very essence of its spirit; evoking the mood of reverent yet discriminating enthusiasm in which all great poetry is best approached.

The study of poetry of our own time has one special advantage and more than one difficulty of its own. We are spared the labour of making ourselves acquainted with the language, history, and ideas of another age, which in the case of older poets is a necessary preparation if we wish to gain true insight into the poet's mind. The language of present-day poets is our language; the ideas which surround them surround us also; many words and allusions that later on will call for the note of explanation, are a plain tale to us; we are free to go straight to the heart of the matter, and find out the interpretation offered to us by the seers of our common life.

One great difficulty in the way of the contemporaries of a great poet lies in the fact that the more original he is, the less possible it can be for him to be immediately understood. We are accustomed to gird at the obtuseness of an age that paid twelve pounds for *Paradise Lost*, or turned a deaf ear and stolid back upon Wordsworth; but after all, if ordinary minds lived in a state of such ready apprehension as to find nothing strange in the utterances of genius, there would be little need for the revealing power of the great poets at all, and less for the aureole of mingled wonder and admiration that rests upon one whose place among the sacred bards has won its recognition.

In this respect students of Victorian poetry at the present moment are again fortunate. It is now more than sixty years since Lord Tennyson's first poems were published, and nearly sixty years since Mr. Browning's *Pauline* appeared. The time of indifference or sarcasm that greeted both poets is already safely gone by; no denser medium than our own mental equipment stands between us and what they have to teach.

An opposite danger is that of making too much of our own age and all that pertains to it. So far as regards the future it would be waste time to speculate upon this possibility; but we do need to be on our guard lest an over estimate of our modern poetry should steal away any of our will or ability to burn candles at the older shrines. Not that our individual estimate signifies to the poets, whose 'life and use and name and fame' are in safe keeping; but it signifies intensely to ourselves; and those among us who have a sincere desire not only to know what we like, but to 'approve things that *are* excellent,' know how difficult it is to attain to a sure and clear judgment concerning them. Here indeed we are brought face to face with a crucial difficulty in the study of all poetry and all art. In the study of recent poetry we are not helped over it so well as might be expected from the fact that the genius of our century has been so earnestly directed to criticism, because on examination it turns out that divergences of judgment among the leading critics are many, and not unfrequently very serious. There is indeed no royal road to a just judgment; we must be content to move along quietly, laying aside here a prejudice, and there, it may be, an early favourite ; gaining now a new perception of beauty, now a glimpse along vistas of meaning hitherto concealed ; the object of our care not being to improve our taste and end as the fastidious connoisseur, but to enter into poetry as an end in itself; or, it may be, to become more capable of sharing in a higher and fuller life than our own, through looking at life as with the eyes of those who have seen it most truly, and have most wisely measured the relative values of its elements.

Constant companionship with the poets themselves is the best school. The great poet, it has been said, ' is his own best critic ; his noblest conception and mightiest line are the strictest censors of his faulty phrase or unworthy thought.' [1] And again, just as we can detect shortcomings in the appointments of a room by imagining some noble work of art—picture or statue—set in the midst of it, so we may, as Matthew Arnold has shown, try poetry as we read it by test lines of unquestioned perfection. Only here too, judgment is needed in the application of our tests, or we may find ourselves breaking butterflies upon the wheel.

But it would be a great pity to neglect the minor poetry altogether. It is almost certain that many readers miss the enjoyment and enlightenment that might be theirs in the

[1] *Poetry and Life* : Inaugural Address by A. C. Bradley, M.A., Professor of English Literature in the University of Glasgow.

realms of poetry, because they feel bound to begin at once upon the great works whose names are in all mouths, and finding themselves unable to cope with these, give up poetry altogether, perhaps with an unacknowledged sense of relief, perhaps with a slight feeling of self-contempt. Easier poems and easier writers to begin with, might have led them on to a very different conclusion. The Victorian era is rich in lesser poets, of whom each adds something that we would not as yet willingly lose.

A word or two about the use of such books as Mr. Robertson's *Analysis of 'In Memoriam'* and Mrs. Sutherland Orr's *Handbook to the Poetry of Robert Browning* may not be out of place. Students who intend to take their poetry seriously, will find it a good plan to read their poem first very carefully, going over it again and again if necessary, till the leading idea seems quite plain; then, *and not before*, to look at the book's summary and compare their own result with it, returning to the poem itself for confirmation, or for decision if the results differ. Used in this way, not to save thinking but to test it, such aids may be of great service in the mastery of difficult poems.

The chapters in this little book are of course merely preparatory to the much fuller and more detailed study encouraged by attendance on a course of Lectures. But it is only the poet himself who 'doth not only show the way, but giveth so sweete a prospect into the way, as will intice any man to enter into it.'

VICTORIAN POETS.

I. ALFRED TENNYSON.

'The peereless Poet . . . commeth to you with words sent in delightfull proportion, either accompanied with or prepared for the well in-chaunting skill of Musicke; and with a tale forsooth he commeth unto you : with a tale which holdeth children from play, and old men from the chimney corner.'—SIR PHILIP SIDNEY, *Apologie for Poetrie*.

THE very early poems of a great poet are commonly more interesting because they are his than because they are poems ; and perhaps *Mariana* is the only one of Lord Tennyson's earliest publications to be counted amongst the exceptions to this rule. Most readers would have found it hard to forecast from *Oriana, The Merman, The Owl, Circumstance*, that a consummate artist in verse, a profound interpreter of life, a great lyric poet, had arisen. But look-ing back now with this knowledge safely in our possession it is a pleasant task to trace in a line here and a stanza there, in the turn of a thought or the choice of a subject, the first signs of characteristics marked and perfected in the later work.

One of the most remarkable of these is to be found in a poem called by the curious name, *Confessions of a Second-rate*

Mind not at Unity with Itself, for this is the very first of that fine group of modern poems which Tennyson and others after him have devoted to the inner strivings and questionings of the mind that has lost faith in received creeds and doctrines yet clings to the spiritual essence of religion. The longing for a conviction apparently unattainable ; the pain-stricken regret for lost simplicity of faith ; the brave recognition that faith cannot be forced in a nature driven by the spirit to toss amongst doubts and fears as irresistibly as the tempest-driven sea must rage and moan ; all these, the thoughts afterwards so much more fully and richly worked out, are there in embryo, and so, too, is the faint promise of a final note of triumph.

> ' It is man's privilege to doubt,
>   If so be that from doubt at length,
>   Truth may stand forth unmoved of change.'

In another of these ' Early Poems ' there is a suggestion of the coming *Palace of Art* in the *Character* who

> ' stood aloof from other minds
>   In impotence of fancied power.'

There is a further foretaste of subtlety and strength in the *Poet's* inheritance—

> ' Dower'd with the hate of hate, the scorn of scorn,
>   The love of love ; '

and more than a foretaste in the *Ode to Memory* of the vivid pictures of landscape that Lord Tennyson's words excel in calling up—

> ' Come from the woods that belt the gray hill-side,
>   The seven elms, the poplars four
>   That stand beside my father's door,
>   And chiefly from the brook that loves

To purl o'er matted cress and ribbed sand,
Or dimple in the dark of rushy coves,
Drawing into his narrow earthen urn,
    In every elbow and turn,
The filter'd tribute of the rough woodland.'

Mariana's dreary solitude in her decaying grange shows not
only this picturing skill, but also the use which Tennyson often
makes of it to heighten, by the setting of natural description,
the sense of the human *mood* to which he is giving expression.
Mariana herself might have felt quite as forlorn and deserted
in a trim house and sunny, well-kept garden ; but how much
less vividly we should have realised it !

'About a stone-cast from the wall
    A sluice with blacken'd waters slept,
And o'er it many, round and small,
    The cluster'd marish-mosses crept.
Hard by a poplar shook alway,
    All silver green, with gnarled bark :
For leagues no other tree did mark
The level waste, the rounding gray.
        She only said, " My life is dreary,
            He cometh not," she said ;
        She said, " I am aweary, aweary,
            I would that I were dead."

'And ever when the moon was low,
    And the shrill winds were up and away,
In the white curtain, to and fro,
    She saw the gusty shadow sway.
But when the moon was very low,
    And wild winds bound within their cell,
    The shadow of the poplar fell
Upon her bed, across her brow.
        She only said, " The night is dreary,
            He cometh not," she said ;
        She said, " I am aweary, aweary,
            I would that I were dead." '

The beautiful and finished poems of the next two divisions of Lord Tennyson's works fall naturally into several different groups, each of them marking a distinct line in the wide and varied range of his poetry. But before dwelling in turn upon the most important of these groups, with the later developments that spring out of them, it may be well to notice two leading characteristics which from this time onwards pervade the whole of Tennyson's work, whether slight or important.

The first is the *style*, the language, and versification. No one is more keenly alive to the difficulty of expression in 'matter-moulded forms of speech'; but few have so effectually subdued this stubborn medium of language to their will. Lord Tennyson has set a new standard of perfection in technical excellence ; his own art is so perfect that we, simply as readers, rarely notice or think about it at all,—when every word seems just what it should be, we are led along in happy unconsciousness of effort, and are even apt to be a little blinded to the power of his work by its faultless · execution. Yet Tennyson never for a moment sacrifices meaning to sensuous effect ; indeed, his assured hand is shown quite as much in reticence as in his employ-ment of the words and images that go to produce the felicitous result. But his instinct for words of which not only the sound, but the associations help the thought, though quite unobtrusively, enable him to communicate subtleties of meaning, moods of impalpable delicacy, such as in the hands of a smaller genius must have remained amongst the 'fancies that broke through language, and escaped'; and to clothe in noble and appealing forms ideas or feelings widely shared with him by others. As Lowell has justly observed—

> ' Though old the thought and oft exprest,
>   'Tis his at last who says it best ; '

and for us Lord Tennyson has said many things best.
Many a writer, from Dante and Chaucer onwards, has
touched upon the sting of bitterness added to a present
grief by the memory of bygone joy ; but for English hearts
that pain seems now uttered once for all in the grave beauty
of Tennyson's line—

> ' A sorrow's crown of sorrow is remembering happier things.'

Sometimes the whole essence of a poem is compressed
into a single musical line ;

> ' Give us long rest or death, dark death, or dreamful ease.'

His choice or invention of metres is equally happy.
Observe, for example, how the changing metres of *Maud*
suit the ever-varying moods of the singer ; or again how
perfectly the peculiar quatrain stanza of *In Memoriam*
harmonises with the sustained tone of grave sorrow, yet
never becomes monotonous. In this last case there is an
easy means at hand of proving to ourselves how the mind of
a great poet stamps the form adopted with its own unique
character ; the same metre as used by Rossetti in *My
Sister's Sleep* produces such an entirely different effect.
Read three stanzas from each—

> ' The time draws near the birth of Christ ;
>   The moon is hid, the night is still ;
>   A single church below the hill
>   Is pealing, folded in the mist.

> ' A single peal of bells below,
>   That wakens at this hour of rest
>   A single murmur in the breast,
>   That these are not the bells I know.

' Like strangers' voices here they sound,
        In lands where not a memory strays,
        Nor landmark breathes of other days,
But all is new unhallow'd ground.'

                                        In Memoriam.

' She fell asleep on Christmas Eve,
        At length the long ungranted shade
        Of weary eyelids overweigh'd
The pain nought else might yet relieve.

                *   *   *

' Without, there was a cold moon up,
        Of winter radiance sheer and thin ;
        The hollow halo it was in
Was like an icy crystal cup.

                *   *   *

' Twelve struck.   That sound by dwindling years
        Heard in each hour, crept off ; and then
        The ruffled silence spread again,
Like water that a pebble stirs.'

                                        My Sister's Sleep.

Close examination of the distribution of pauses, accents,
alliteration, exhibit the poet's technical skill, but through
and beyond all this there remains the indefinable something,
not to be analysed nor described, but only *felt*, which
distinguishes the style of one original poet from another.
Even the old-established English metre, the ten-syllabled
blank verse, takes a new character as Lord Tennyson shapes
it to his purpose.

        ' So all day long the noise of battle roll'd
        Among the mountains, by the winter sea.'

        ' " I heard the water lapping on the crag,
        And the long ripple washing in the reeds." '

It would be impossible to mistake that for the blank verse
of Milton or Cowper or Wordsworth or Shelley.

Lord Tennyson has another inexhaustible resource in his knowledge of nature and the varied uses he can make of it. It is simple truth that no other poet has brought to his work such a naturalist's powers of minute observation, an endowment of knowledge so wide and so lovingly accurate in detail. Many of his innumerable nature-touches may easily escape the hasty reader, or even a careful reader, who knows little of nature at first hand, so delicate are they; but they provide a rich mine for the lover of nature. Tennyson's attitude towards these things is quite different from Wordsworth's; to him the meanest flowers that blow do not give 'thoughts that do often lie too deep for tears'; but he takes such pure joy in the things themselves for their own sakes that the reader must be very dull indeed of soul who is not led to enjoy them also. And not a few of us will furthermore be led to wonder at our own contrasting blindness. How many will undertake to say for certain, without purposely looking to see, the number of divisions into which the green case of a horse-chestnut splits when the nut is ripe?—a sight we must all have had before our eyes scores of times. Tennyson makes no parade whatever of telling us such things; he always seems to take it for granted that his own store of knowledge is common property, and constantly uses such details in illustration as being the most familiar matters of every-day experience by which to explain the less known. In this case he incidentally describes the colour of auburn hair—

> 'In gloss and hue the chestnut when the shell
> Divides three-fold to show the fruit within.'

Readers of Mrs. Gaskell's delightful story, *Cranford*, will thank me for reminding them of the remarkable passage where Miss Matty's whilom lover, the rough-spoken, true-hearted farmer, Mr. Holbrook, dwells with such self-shamed delight on the famous 'black as ash-buds in March,' or the cedar's 'layers of shade.' Is there any other poet who has noticed, or at least recorded, the change in the lark's song as he nears 'his happy home, the ground'?

> 'Realms of upland, prodigal in oil
> And hoary to the wind.'—*Palace of Art.*

'Hoary to the wind.' How the silver-backed, gray-green olive leaves wave before us at the words! Here is the effect of an ill-natured woman—

> 'All my heart turn'd from her as a thorn
> Turns from the sea.'

The snowdrop has been utilised as an emblem of purity perhaps more than enough; but it is Tennyson who observes that the comparison is truest of the *green* in the flower—

> 'Pure as the lines of green that streak the white
> Of the first snowdrop's inner leaves.'— *The Princess.*

And when the destruction of life amongst wild animals has to be mentioned, the time-honoured tiger and spider give way to strikingly fresh instances—

> 'The Mayfly is torn by the swallow, the sparrow spear'd by
> the shrike.'—*Maud.*

That the shrike, or 'butcher-bird,' impales flies, bees, and tiny birds on thorns near its nest for the gradual service of its own young, is by no means a matter of general knowledge even yet.

To Lord Tennyson the time of year—

> 'When rosy plumelets tuft the larch ;'.

or,—

> 'To-night the winds begin to rise
>   And roar from yonder dropping day :
>   The last red leaf is whirled away,
> The rooks are blown about the skies ; '

the hour of the day,—

> 'Risest thou thus, dim dawn, again,
>   And howlest, issuing out of night,
>   With blasts that blow the poplar white,
> And lash with storm the streaming pane.'
>   *In Memoriam.*

> ' The hour
> When the thick-moted sunbeam lay
> Athwart the chambers, and the day
> Was sloping toward his western bower ;'—*Mariana.*

or of the night,—

> ' Nigh upon that hour
> When the lone hern forgets his melancholy,
> Lets down his other leg, and stretching, dreams
> Of goodly supper in the distant pool ;'—*Gareth and Lynette.*

are all best registered in terms of nature. Sheer grief at
the notion of leaving her ever-fresh life is one of the
strongest deterrents that warn the tempted one in *The Two
Voices* from suicide, and this even when the tempter carefully points out the quiet indifference of Nature to the
presence of her admirer—

> 'I wept, " Tho' I should die, I know
> That all about the thorn will blow
> In tufts of rosy-tinted snow."
>
> *   *   *   *   *
>
> ' " Not less the bee would range her cells,
> The furzy prickle fire the dells,
> The foxglove cluster dappled bells." ' '

The same thought reappears in a softened form in the *May Queen*—

> 'The building rook 'll caw from the windy tall elm-tree,
> And the tufted plover pipe along the fallow lea,
> And the swallow 'ill come back again with summer o'er the wave,
> But I shall lie alone, mother, within the mouldering grave.'

A still closer and more intimate affection breathes through the delicately-rendered sense of forsakenness imputed to trees and brook when he to whom they were dear is gone away—

> 'Unwatch'd the garden bough shall sway,
>   The tender blossom flutter down,
>   Unlov'd, that beech will gather brown,
> This maple burn itself away;
>
> 'Unlov'd, the sun-flower, shining fair,
>   Ray round with flames her disk of seed,
>   And many a rose-carnation feed
> With summer spice the humming air;
>
> 'Unlov'd, by many a sandy bar,
>   The brook shall babble down the plain,
>   At noon or when the lesser wain
> Is twisting round the polar star;
>
> 'Uncar'd for, gird the windy grove,
>   And flood the haunts of hern and crake;
>   Or into silver arrows break
> The sailing moon in creek and cove.'

To match the sentiment of those, one must go to the pathetic last writing of poor Richard Jefferies:—'I wonder to myself how they can all get on without me; how they manage, bird and flower, without ME, to keep the calendar for them. For I noted it so carefully and lovingly day by day. . . . They go on without me, orchis-flower and cowslip. I cannot number them all. I hear, as it were, the

patter of their feet—flower and buds, and the beautiful
clouds that go over, with the sweet rush of rain and burst of
sun glory among the leafy trees. They go on, and I am no
more than the least of the empty shells that strew the sward
of the hill.'

But with all his love, Tennyson is no stranger to the
terrible, inexorable side of Nature, and the deep misgivings
it can induce as to human destiny. He does not, like
Wordsworth, find Nature the very interpreter of God, find
immortality 'to one who lives among the mountains a
perfectly plain tale'; but he wins his way to that solemn
faith in love and the victory of love *in spite of* Nature
through a conflict in which Nature as an enemy

> 'red in tooth and claw
> With ravine, shrieked against his creed.'

Yet when the victory is won, this vanquished enemy is
folded safely within the embrace of an all-conquering faith
in

> 'One far-off divine event
> To which the whole creation moves.'

Often some object of nature or landscape, ordinary enough
in itself, is wonderfully moulded into the vehicle of emotion ;
as in that most beautiful of lyrics—

> 'Break, break, break,
>   On thy cold gray stones, O Sea !
> And I would that my tongue could utter
>   The thoughts that arise in me.
>
> 'O well for the fisherman's boy,
>   That he shouts with his sister at play !
> O well for the sailor lad,
>   That he sings in his boat on the bay !

> ' And the stately ships go on,
>   To their haven under the hill ;
>   But O for the touch of a vanish'd hand,
>   And the sound of a voice that is still !

> ' Break, break, break,
>   At the foot of thy crags, O Sea !
>   But the tender grace of a day that is dead
>   Will never come back to me.'

There, in some mysterious way, the very sea and crags breathe out the dumb grief, the ineffable sadness and longing of the man's heart. This strangely expressive interweaving of thought and scenery is particularly noticeable all through *In Memoriam.*

Returning now to the two divisions of short poems, perhaps the first to attract attention are the simple idylls, such as *The Miller's Daughter* and *The Gardener's Daughter.* In pure idyllic poetry—that is, as the word itself signifies, picture-making poetry—Lord Tennyson surpasses all our other poets ; his numbers of delicately wrought descriptions of country scenes, rustic life, and natural effects stand by themselves in their truth, their grace of subject and language, and in the vividness with which the scene described is placed, as it seems, before the reader's very eyes. Take the *Lady of Shalott's* island—

> ' On either side the river lie
>   Long fields of barley and of rye,
>   That clothe the wold and meet the sky ;
>   And thro' the field the road runs by
>   To many-tower'd Camelot ;
>   And up and down the people go,
>   Gazing where the lilies blow
>   Round an island there below,
>   The island of Shalott.

'Willows whiten, aspens quiver,
   Little breezes dusk and shiver
Thro' the wave that runs for ever
By the island in the river
      Flowing down to Camelot.
Four gray walls, and four gray towers,
Overlook a space of flowers,
And the silent isle imbowers
      The Lady of Shalott.'

Or take one of Œnone's song-plaints—

'For now the noonday quiet holds the hill :
The grasshopper is silent in the grass :
The lizard, with his shadow on the stone,
Rests like a shadow, and the winds are dead.'

Or hear the mill-stream in that happy story of love both
sudden and lasting, *The Miller's Daughter*—

'Or from the bridge I lean'd to hear
   The mill-dam rushing down with noise,
And see the minnows everywhere
   In crystal eddies glance and poise,
The tall flag-flowers when they sprung
   Below the range of stepping-stones,
Or those three chestnuts near, that hung
   In masses thick with milky cones.
      *   *   *   *
'I loved the brimming wave that swam
   Thro' quiet meadows round the mill,
The sleepy pool above the dam,
   The pool beneath it never still,
The meal-sacks on the whiten'd floor,
   The dark round of the dripping wheel,
The very air about the door,
   Made misty with the floating meal.'

In the first edition of this poem it was the plunge of a
water-rat that was followed by the vision of Alice's face
reflected in the water, and nothing could better mark the

delicate sense of harmony to be learnt from Tennyson
than the change of even that slight disturbance to the
absolutely peaceful—

> ' Then leapt a trout. In lazy mood
>   I watch'd the little circles die ;
> They past into the level flood,
>   And there a vision caught my eye.'

Nor are his skill and fancy confined to English scenes :
the half mystic, dreamy land of the Lotos-eaters ; the
gorgeous, scorching tropics are just as tellingly delineated—

> A land of streams ! some, like a downward smoke,
> Slow-dropping veils of thinnest lawn, did go ;
> And some thro' wavering lights and shadows broke,
> Rolling a slumbrous sheet of foam below.
> They saw the gleaming river seaward flow
> From the inner land : far off, three mountain-tops,
> Three silent pinnacles of aged snow,
> Stood sunset-flush'd ; and, dew'd with showery drops,
> Up-clomb the shadowy pine above the woven copse.'
>   *The Lotos-Eaters.*

> No sail from day to day, but every day
> The sunrise broken into scarlet shafts
> Among the palms and ferns and precipices ;
> The blaze upon the waters to the east ;
> The blaze upon his island overhead ;
> The blaze upon the waters to the west ;
> Then the great stars that globed themselves in Heaven,
> The hollower-bellowing ocean, and again
> The scarlet shafts of sunrise—but no sail.'—*Enoch Arden.*

The sea fragments, too, scattered up and down, would
make a delightful study in themselves—

> ' One show'd an iron coast, and angry waves.
>   You seem'd to hear them climb and fall
> And roar rock-thwarted under bellowing caves,
>   Beneath the windy wall.'—*Palace of Art.*

'The plunging seas draw backward from the land
  Their moon-led waters white.'—*Palace of Art.*

'Bluster the winds and tides the self-same way,
  Crisp foam-flakes scud along the level sand,
Torn from the fringe of spray.'—*Dream of Fair Women.*

'Rounded by the stillness of the beach
To where the bay runs up its latest horn.
  We left the dying ebb that faintly lipp'd
The flat red granite.'—*Audley Court.*

'Listening now to the tide in its broad-flung shipwrecking roar,
  Now to the scream of a madden'd beach dragg'd down by the waves.'
                                           Maud.

It will be noticed that Tennyson rarely pictures rugged,
barren wildness. That he *can* do it, one stanza in the
Palace of Art is sufficient witness—

'And one a foreground black with stones and slags,
  Beyond, a line of heights, and higher
All barr'd with long white cloud the scornful crags,
  And highest, snow and fire ; '

but clearly he prefers the rich lands of cultivation ; woods,
streams, many-flowered hedgerows, stretches of grassy
meadows ; and in their delineation he works in touch after
touch, yet all strictly subdued with sure eye to the whole,
till his own picture has the same unconfused richness of
effect.

That well-known favourite, *The Brook*, is perhaps in its
own way as perfect an instance as any.

'I come from haunts of coot and hern,
  I make a sudden sally,
And sparkle out among the fern,
  To bicker down a valley.

'By thirsty hills I hurry down,
  Or slip between the ridges,
By twenty thorps, a little town,
  And half a hundred bridges.

'Till last by Philip's farm I flow
  To join the brimming river,
For men may come and men may go,
  But I go on for ever.

'I chatter over stony ways,
  In little sharps and trebles,
I bubble into eddying bays,
  I babble on the pebbles.

'With many a curve my banks I fret,
  By many a field and fallow,
And many a fairy foreland set
  With willow-weed and mallow.

'I chatter, chatter, as I flow
  To join the brimming river,
For men may come and men may go,
  But I go on for ever.

'I wind about, and in and out,
  With here a blossom sailing,
And here and there a lusty trout,
  And here and there a grayling.

'And here and there a foamy flake
  Upon me, as I travel
With many a silver waterbreak
  Above the golden gravel,

'And draw them all along, and flow
  To join the brimming river,
For men may come and men may go,
  But I go on for ever.

'I steal by lawns and grassy plots,
  I slide by hazel covers ;
I move the sweet forget-me-nots
  That grow for happy lovers.

'I slip, I slide, I gloom, I glance,
   Among my skimming swallows;
I make the netted sunbeam dance
   Against my sandy shallows.

'I murmur under moon and stars
   In brambly wildernesses;
I linger by my shingly bars;
   I loiter round my cresses;

'And out again I curve and flow
   To join the brimming river,
For men may come and men may go,
   But I go on for ever.'

To let that have its will with one's mind is almost as
good and refreshing as actually to lie on the sun-warmed
banks by 'haunts of coot and hern,' listening to this tinkling
chatter in the original. It shows too the minute detail in
Tennyson's work. At every break in the song one would
suppose the brook's whole character had been given; yet
another and another and another touch is added, each
perfectly fresh, and impossible to be spared when once it
has been heard. And finally the way in which sound fits
sense is in itself no small marvel. We have only to alter a
word here and there—to read, say, 'edges' for 'pebbles'
in the last line of stanza four, or 'flying' for 'skimming'
in the second line of stanza eleven—to realise instantly the
subtle dependence of the brook-prattle on having every
syllable precisely right in sound as well as meaning.

Pure idylls shade off into narrative poems equally simple
and graceful in style, artistic in construction, and full of
human interest and feeling. *Dora*, *Godiva*, *The Lord of
Burleigh*, belong to this group, of which *Enoch Arden* is
the later and most important poem. So touching is this
last in its sweetness and its sorrow, in the tragic destiny

deepened by the very virtues of the three constant hearts
whom disaster overtakes, that, as another poet has said,
'it appears to spring from the very fountain of tears.'

There are again two or three striking dramatic pieces,
giving voice to the strange half-crazed ecstasy of St.
Simeon Stylites on his pillar of torture ; or to the shrinking
terror of Tithonus in the face of his self-invoked fate of
deathless, unceasing decay ; or to the restless craving
of the aged Ulysses, wearied to death of his humdrum
home existence, to return to a life of heroic adventure—and
determined to do it.

> ' How dull it is to pause, to make an end,
>   To rust unburnish'd, not to shine in use !
>   As tho' to breathe were life.
>
>   *   *   *
>
> 'Death closes all : but something ere the end,
>   Some work of noble note, may yet be done,
>   Not unbecoming men that strove with Gods.
>
>   *   *   *   *
>
> ' Tho' much is taken, much abides ; and tho'
>   We are not now that strength which in old days
>   Moved earth and heaven ; that which we are, we are ;
>   One equal temper of heroic hearts,
>   Made weak by time and fate, but strong in will
>   To strive, to seek, to find, and not to yield.'

In these dramatic lyrics we see the forerunners of Lord
Tennyson's dramas ; but when we turn to the dramas, the
first thing that strikes us is the predominance of thought
and feeling over action. Thrown on a time of changing
opinions, scientific discoveries, political and social advances,
he has shown himself a true son of his age. And as his
chief interest is in thoughts, opinions, feelings, so his
work is happiest when carried out in lyrical form rather

than when it requires the connected action and forward movement of regular drama. His readers have to admit that *Harold*, *Becket*, and even *Queen Mary*, have far less fire and inspiration than the lyrical poetry, and are much less characteristic and successful than the dramatic rendering of a single mood, or, as in the 'monodrama' of *Maud*, of successive and varying moods in a single mind. Dramatic presentations of .this kind occur from time to time all through the Laureate's work, and are always striking. One naturally thinks first of the two *Northern Farmers*, especially him of the old style, with the clear glimpse given into the mind of the man, narrow, prejudiced, clouded with ignorance, yet faithful to such lights as shone dimly upon him ; staunch in discharge of duties to land, squire, parson, and child ; and no less firmly determined not to be balked of his routine glass of ale by any decrees, whether doctor's or coming from the hazily-apprehended 'godamoighty.'

> ' What atta stannin' theer fur, an' doesn bring ma the aäle ?
> Doctor's a 'toättler, lass, an a's hallus i' the owd taäle ;
> I weänt breäk rules fur Doctor, a knaws naw moor nor a floy ;
> Git ma my aäle I tell tha', an' if I mun doy I mun doy.'

Perhaps we shall find even more pathos in the *Grandmother's* lightly-strung reminiscences when the news comes to her of her eldest son's death—

> ' Why do you look at me, Annie ? you think I am hard and cold ;
> But all my children have gone before me, I am so old :
> I cannot weep for Willy, nor can I weep for the rest ;
> Only at your age, Annie, I could have wept with the best.
>
>   *   *   *   *   *
>
> ' Pattering over the boards, my Annie who left me at two,
> Patter she goes, my own little Annie, an Annie like you :
> Pattering over the boards, she comes and goes at her will,
> While Harry is in the five-acre and Charlie ploughing the hill.
>
>   *   *   *   *   *

> ' So Willy has gone, my beauty, my eldest-born, my flower ;
> But how can I weep for Willy, he has but gone for an hour,—
> Gone for a minute, my son, from this room into the next ;
> I, too, shall go in a minute. What time have I to be vext ?'

The finest of all, to my own mind, is *Rizpah*, with its passion of enduring mother's love, stronger than death, stronger than the mighty powers of superstitious dread, the love that goes out by night through storm and darkness to gather the bones of the gibbeted son as they fall one by one, hoarding them for secret burial in holy ground.

> ' Why should he call me to-night, when he knows that I cannot go?
> For the downs are as bright as day, and the full moon stares at the snow.

> ' We should be seen, my dear ; they would spy us out of the town.
> The loud black nights for us, and the storm rushing over the down,
> When I cannot see my own hand, but am led by the creak of the chain,
> And grovel and grope for my son till I find myself drenched with the rain.
>   *   *   *   *   *
> ' Do you think I was scared by the bones? I kiss'd 'em, I buried 'em all—
> I can't dig deep, I am old—in the night by the churchyard wall.
> My Willy 'ill rise up whole when the trumpet of judgment 'ill sound,
> But I charge you never to say that I laid him in holy ground.'

When we compare such emotion as this, on the one hand with the fierce passions of Queen Mary in the drama (excepting the one lyrical outburst wrung from Mary in her extremity of despair), and on the other hand with the indescribable beauty of such songs as that in *The Princess* about the sad, strange ' days that are no more,' with the mixed feelings that remembrance of them brings—

> ' Deep as first love, and wild with all regret,'

it becomes evident at once that the more closely Lord
Tennyson's forms of verse approach forms ' prepared for
the well-inchaunting skill of musicke,' the finer is their
effect.

It has already been remarked how deeply Tennyson
has shared in the many interests of his time, a fact which
more than anything else has helped to make him not only
a great poet, but the great representative poet of his age,
our spokesman amongst the immortals.   Lord Tennyson
began to write just at the time when the great democratic
movement which has taken place in England during this
century was beginning its struggle with the older system of
privilege, exclusion, and class-dominance.   His early poems
were published a short time before the Reform Bill of 1832,
the first considerable success of the reforming party.   He
has told us himself how eagerly he and the band of under-
graduate friends who were proud to count Arthur Hallam
their leader, threw themselves into the great questions of
which men's minds were full ; how in the stately old college

> '. . . we held debate, a band
>   Of youthful friends, on mind and art,
>   And labour, and the changing mart,
> And all the framework of the land.'

His sympathies lay with the liberalism of the type especially
identified with the 'Christian Socialists,' and we find the
glow of that enthusiasm faithfully reflected in his poetry.
More than once a disappointed lover, smarting under the
hard worldliness shown in unhesitating sacrifice of a girl's
happiness to the worship of position, or the coarser worship
of gold, is chosen to pour out vials of wrath upon the
corruptions of a social system just then grasping its power

perhaps all the more fiercely as its dominance was felt to be slipping away. We have in these cases to make due allowance for the dramatic form, especially as regards the actual expressions employed; but a comparison of them with other poems will show how far they do in substance express the poet's own feelings. The rather self-complacent suitor of *Locksley Hall*, not too much cast down to be able to moralise on his cousin's inferior choice, is not to be ranked with Maud's passionate lover, whose mind is shaken to its very foundations by his ill fate; yet they are charged with kindred messages—

'Cursed be the social wants that sin against the strength of youth !
Cursed be the social lies that warp us from the living truth !'

Maud, besides containing some of the most wonderful love-songs that Tennyson ever wrote, is a passionate outbreak against the deadening materialism developed by a long duration of peace and successful commercial enterprise, which reached its climax just before the Crimean War. It is the poet's contribution to an awakening of the national conscience to evils fought by social reformers and philanthropists in their own different ways.

'Why do they prate of the blessings of Peace? we have made them
    a curse,
Pickpockets, each hand lusting for all that is not its own ;
And lust of gain, in the spirit of Cain, is it better or worse
Than the heart of the citizen hissing in war on his own hearthstone ?

*　　*　　*　　*　　*　　*　　*

'When a Mammonite mother kills her babe for a burial fee,
And Timour-Mammon grins on a pile of children's bones,
Is it peace or war? better, war ! loud war by land and by sea,
War with a thousand battles, and shaking a hundred thrones.'

But Tennyson cannot endure lawless attempts to right

even the worst of social wrongs. He carries the love of measure, balance, 'order serviceable,' which has governed all his own work into his views of what social life should be. He utters sincerest disapproval of French extravagances, whether shown in dreams of 'glory' won by warfare—

> 'We love not this French God, the child of Hell,
> Wild War, who breaks the converse of the wise;'

or in internal disorganisation.

> '. . . social truth shall spread,
>   And justice, ev'n tho' thrice again
>   The red fool-fury of the Seine
> Should pile her barricades with dead.'
>
> *In Memoriam.*

> 'But yonder, whiff! there comes a sudden heat,
> The gravest citizen seems to lose his head,
> The king is scared, the soldier will not fight,
> The little boys begin to shoot and stab,
> A kingdom topples over with a shriek
> Like an old woman, and down rolls the world
> In mock heroics stranger than our own.'—*The Princess.*

In this last case the next speaker corrects the too sweeping effect of the lines by the reflection—

> 'Maybe wildest dreams
> Are but the needful preludes of the truth;'

but elsewhere Tennyson has repeatedly condemned the excesses of such preludes. Even out of evil good sometimes works itself, but none the less turbulence remains evil and a thing to be hated.

> 'O shall the braggart shout
> For some blind glimpse of freedom work itself
> Thro' madness, hated by the wise, to law
> System and empire?'—*Love and Duty.*

Not only patriotism, but genuine and sympathetic admiration lead him to speak so lovingly of the land, with all her
faults—

> 'Where Freedom slowly broadens down
> From precedent to precedent.'

> 'That sober freedom out of which there springs
> Our loyal passion for our temperate kings.'

> 'Our slowly-grown
> And crown'd Republic's crowning common sense.'

His ideal has always been the time of which he questions—

> 'Ah ! when shall all men's good
> Be each man's rule, and universal Peace
> Lie like a shaft of light across the land ?'

But his burning hatred of tyranny and social injustice, his
patriotic conviction that our own country is the land where
they have been met and overcome by the manliest and best
sort of opposition, never for a moment blind him to the
shortcomings of undisciplined, ignorant numbers. In his
fine *Ode on the Death of the Duke of Wellington* all sense
of the conservative opposition which the Duke as a
statesman had offered to democratic reform bills is completely sunk in the tribute to his magnificent services in the
cause of 'sober freedom,' and the cause of the discipline
and order imperatively needed to

> ' . . . drill the raw world for the march of mind,
> Till crowds at length be sane, and crowns be just.'

He feels keenly that 'knowledge comes but wisdom
lingers,' and fears the dangers to be expected when knowledge, unguided by wisdom, seizes upon power.

> ' Let her know her place ;
> She is the second, not the first.

> 'A higher hand must make her mild,
>   If all be not in vain, and guide
>   Her footsteps, moving side by side
> With Wisdom, like the younger child.'

And he frequently urges that need for Reverence which it is the undeniable tendency of modern democracies to lose sight of.

> 'Make Knowledge circle with the winds ;
>   But let her herald, Reverence, fly
>   Before her to whatever sky
> Bear seed of men and growth of mind.'

> 'Let knowledge grow from more to more,
>   But more of reverence in us dwell.'

> 'Self-reverence, self-knowledge, self-control,
>   These three alone lead life to sovereign power.'

True freedom, he holds, lies in willing obedience to duty, and to the dictates of just and enlightened laws, and he who thus submits—

> 'Shall find the toppling crags of Duty scaled
>   Are close upon the shining table-lands
>   To which our God Himself is moon and sun.'

It is not surprising that with the success of many aims of the liberalism of sixty years ago, Lord Tennyson's convictions should have passed on into the conservatism reflected in *Locksley Hall Sixty Years After*.

The same love of law, but of progressive and ennobled law, is apparent when Tennyson deals with the social position of women in *The Princess*, that curious 'medley' of laughter and gravity, of mock-heroism and serious poetry. The Lady Ida's revolt fails through its overstrained absoluteness ; but the poem anticipates many a modification actually won since then, and concludes with an idealising of relations noble enough to satisfy the high-spirited princess herself.

> ' The woman's cause is man's : they rise or sink
>   Together, dwarf'd or godlike, bond or free :
> 　　　　*　　　　*　　　　*　　　　*　　　　*
>   For woman is not undevelopt man,
>   But diverse : could we make her as the man,
>   Sweet Love were slain ; his dearest bond is this,
>   Not like to like, but like in difference.
>   Yet in the long years liker must they grow ;
>   The man be more of woman, she of man ;
>   He gain in sweetness and in moral height,
>   Nor lose the wrestling thews that throw the world ;
>   She mental breadth, nor fail in childward care,
>   Nor lose the childlike in the larger mind ;
>   Till at the last she set herself to man,
>   Like perfect music unto noble words ;
>   And so these twain, upon the skirts of Time,
>   Sit side by side, full-summ'd in all their powers,
>   Dispensing harvest, sowing the To-be,
>   Self-reverent each and reverencing each,
>   Distinct in individualities,
>   But like each other ev'n as those who love.'

Still more deeply wrought into the very texture of
Tennyson's poetry is his treatment of moral and religious
problems in the light of that new appeal to the underlying
principles of spiritual faith best represented in theology by
Frederick Maurice, and in philosophy by the late Professor
T. H. Green.　Not by the methods of the theologian or
philosopher, but in the way of the true poet, whose glory it
is to divine and exhibit the ' soul of good in things evil,'
Tennyson passes on from the first doubts and distractions
of the ' mind not at unity with itself' to his final conviction
that

> ' All is well, tho' faith and form
>   Be sunder'd in the night of fear ; '

entering as he goes into the subtlest and most crucial
questions of morals and religion raised in a time of penetrat-

ing inquiry. It is impossible to do more here than indicate in the shortest way where some of these deep thinkings are best to be studied.

The Two Voices is a balanced contest between a sense of the misery and bitterness in human life, so keen as to bring with it the temptation to self-destruction, and a slowly victorious sense not only of its brighter side, but of a possible meaning in *all*, which makes endurance the gladder as well as the wiser part. The tempter's scoff loses its sting as the craving of the tempted for 'more life and fuller' gains its way.

> 'Here sits he shaping wings to fly :
> His heart forbodes a mystery :
> He names the name Eternity.'

The Palace of Art exhibits at its strongest the besetting danger to the highly cultivated of selfish exclusiveness, of living in a lofty isolation which seems to grant release from common beliefs, common laws of conduct, and sanctions contemptuous disdain for the multitude. The soul sitting on Godlike heights, surrounded by every noble and beautiful work that the world could produce, announces at last—

> 'I take possession of man's mind and deed.
> I care not what the sects may brawl.
> I sit as God holding no form of creed,
> But contemplating all.'

She is suddenly awakened.

> 'Lest she should fail and perish utterly,
> God, before whom ever lie bare
> The abysmal deeps of Personality,
> Plagued her with sore despair.'

She passes through a time of deep and wholesome distress, and then the truth dawns that her way of salvation lies not in renunciation of enjoyment, but in *shared* enjoyment, purified from selfishness.

> ' " Make me a cottage in the vale," she said,
>   " Where I may mourn and pray.
>
> ' " Yet pull not down my palace towers that are
>   So lightly, beautifully built :
>   Perchance I may return with others there
>   When I have purged my guilt." '

In *Love and Duty* a more searching question is faced. Two passionate lovers are compelled by duty to part without earthly fulfilment of their love. One of them looks back on the fierce struggle they have come through, and asks what they have gained or lost by their passion and bitter farewell. Is the end of it all only streaming eyes and breaking hearts, solitary broodings over life in ruins ? Not so. In spite of anguish and separation, the answer rings brave and clear—

> ' Am I not the nobler thro' thy love ?
>   O three times less unworthy ! likewise thou
>   Art more thro' Love, and greater than thy years.'

Love has performed its work of enlightenment and discipline ; the lover has courage to do the right, and faces the issue

> ' Most Godlike, being most a man.'

Duty is exalted, yet not after all at the expense of Love,— at their highest they are *not* antagonistic, for it is the very strength and purity of love that demands the sacrifice of itself.

> ' For Love himself took part against himself '

to enforce the law of ' Duty loved of Love.'

The *Vision of Sin* shows the Nemesis of a life of sensuality, and shadows out the far-reaching thought that the sinfulness of sin lies in its being always a matter of choice. The issue is left doubtful, as it must remain until the possibility of choice is over.

> 'At last I heard a voice upon the slope
> Cry to the summit, " Is there any hope ? "
> To which an answer peal'd from that high land,
> But in a tongue no man could understand ;
> And on the glimmering limit far withdrawn
> God made Himself an awful rose of dawn.'

The Higher Pantheism finely utters in poetry the idea that philosophy expresses in saying that the whole is in every part; or religion in saying that the Divine presence is everywhere.

> ' Speak to Him thou for He hears, and Spirit with Spirit can meet—
> Closer is He than breathing, and nearer than hands and feet.'

But all these shorter poems compared with *In Memoriam* are as small porches or ante-chambers to a noble temple. It appeared in 1850, seventeen years after the sudden death at Vienna of Lord Tennyson's closest friend, Arthur H. Hallam. 'Grief,' says Mr. Aubrey de Vere, in the closing lines of a thoughtful sonnet—

> ' Grief should be
> Like joy, majestic, equable, sedate ;
> Confirming, cleansing, raising, making free ;
> Strong to consume small troubles, to commend
> Great thoughts, grave thoughts, thoughts lasting to the end.'

Perhaps the ideal could hardly find a more perfect fulfil-ment than in this wonderful series of poems, as they lead on and up from the first desolating shock of bereavement, through benumbing pains of loss, shadowy fears, doubts raised by science and stern facts, moments of recovered

serenity, musings on here and hereafter, to the final triumph
of love and peace and faith.

> ' O living will that shall endure
>   When all that seems shall suffer shock,
>   Rise in the spiritual rock,
> Flow thro' our deeds and make them pure,
>
> ' That we may lift from out of dust
>   A voice as unto him that hears,
>   A cry above the conquer'd years
> To one that with us works, and trust,
>
> ' With faith that comes of self-control,
>   The truths that never can be proved
>   Until we close with all we loved,
> And all we flow from, soul in soul.'

In Memoriam is not a sermon : it neither preaches nor
argues nor expounds.

> ' If these brief lays, of Sorrow born,
>   Were taken to be such as closed,
>   Grave doubts and answers here proposed,
> Then these were such as men might scorn :
>   *   *   *   *
> ' Nor dare she trust a larger lay,
>   But rather loosens from the lip
>   Short swallow-flights of song, that dip
> Their wings in tears, and skim away.'

But the poem searches deeply; and so long as there are
human hearts pierced with grief, assailed by doubt, failing
for fear, they will find in it hid treasure, and the utterance
that gives relief.

As students of poetry it is needful to ask ourselves
whether the teachings of sorrow have gained reality at the
expense of the poetry,—whether the poet has injured his
art for the sake of his moral.   But perhaps the more closely

In Memoriam is studied, the more certainly that question
will seem to answer itself as soon as asked. Like all high
poetry, *In Memoriam* needs close study; but whether we
test it by comparison with the best elegaic poetry we already
possessed—with Milton's *Lycidas* or Shelley's *Adonais;* or
whether we examine the continuity and completeness of
the whole poem, or observe the perfect finish of each small
canto in itself; whether we dwell on the exquisite pictures
of nature, subdued in tone to fit harmony with the rest, or
on the 'music of perfect language,' in which all finds
utterance, our verdict can hardly be other than—*benedicto
benedicatur*.

Amongst other poems contained in the second and third
divisions, there are several—*The Lady of Shalott, Sir
Galahad, Sir Launcelot and Queen Guinevere,* and above
all, that beautiful fragment, the *Morte d'Arthur,* afterwards
incorporated in the last *Idyll of the King*—that show how
Tennyson's thoughts were already attracted by the Arthurian
legends which were later to give him the materials of his
greatest poem. Between the years 1859 and 1877, the
Idylls of the King appeared by instalments. But delightful
as it was felt to be to welcome each new set of *Idylls* as it
came out, the lasting advantage of being able to read the
poem for the first time as a whole, instead of in fragments,
is far greater. Its real character was for a while disguised
by publication in parts; it seemed to be merely a series of
slightly-connected pictures of Arthur's court and the adventures of his knights; and this misapprehension was
confirmed by the name *Idylls,* especially as the order of
publication was not that of their sequence as a whole, but
the middle parts—*Vivien, Enid, Elaine, Guinevere*—appeared first. Beautiful as these were, taken as separate

although mutually illustrative poems, they suffered by comparison with the perfect workmanship of *In Memoriam ;* it was thought and said that Lord Tennyson's style was less well adapted to narrative, that intellectual interest was to some extent sacrificed to pictorial richness of effect. Now that these, with the *Idylls* given later to the world, are seen to fit each into its own definite place in a larger and coherent whole, and can be studied as parts of what is in fact a great epic poem, it is natural to regard them differently.

In this great epic we have the story of the rise and fall of a kingdom based on righteousness. In the temporary subjugation of force and evil passion to a will strong and holy; in the slipping away from a yoke too noble to be long endured by natures of a baser mould ; in the overthrow amidst gloom and confusion of the high rule ; in the seeming utter failure, which is yet nowhere accepted as final failure ; there is placed before us a spiritual problem of profound interest both in itself and in the way it is handled. We recognise, dimly shadowed in the contests of Arthur and his knights with open foes and false friends, signs of the battle as old as humanity itself, the truceless, never-ended conflict of ' Sense at war with Soul.'

On grounds for which excellent reasons can be given, Tennyson has chosen from the old and often conflicting or even self-contradictory stories of the legendary Arthur, elements capable of being welded into a harmonious character of consistent nobility, purity, and dignity. Let us trace very briefly the course of events recorded in the *Idylls*.

The Coming of Arthur describes the mysterious uncertainty in which his birth—if birth it were—is shrouded.

' From the great deep to the great deep he goes '; and one thing only is certain—the inherent kingliness attested by his deeds, and by his attendants, which wins from King Leodogran consent to Arthur's marriage with Guinevere his daughter and one delight—a consent hastened by the prophetic dream in which Leodogran saw a cloud of mist descend and hide away the earth, but the phantom king of his vision 'stood out in heaven, crown'd.'

Arthur's vow to his best-loved warrior—

> ' " Man's word is God in man :
> Let chance what will, I trust thee to the death ! " '

his vow to the Queen of his choice and his worship—

> ' " Behold, thy doom is mine.
> Let chance what will, I love thee to the death ! " '

are taken ; and his knighthood are bound to himself by vows so stringent and sacred—

> ' That when they rose, knighted from kneeling, some
> Were pale as at the passing of a ghost,
> Some flush'd, and others dazed, as one who wakes
> Half-blinded at the coming of a light.'

The spell of the King's spiritual authority has already asserted itself; in victory and hopefulness his reign begins.

> ' And Arthur and his knighthood for a space
> Were all one will, and thro' that strength the King
> Drew in the petty princedoms under him,
> Fought, and in twelve great battles overcame
> The heathen hordes, and made a realm and reign'd.'

Gareth and Lynette belongs to the early days of happiness. We hear how the mystic City of Camelot, built by the wizard Merlin, rose ; though the fuller description of it is reserved for Galahad's narration—

> ' Like enow
> They are building still, seeing the city is built
> To music, therefore never built at all,
> And therefore built for ever.'

We learn more, too, of the vows by which the Round
Table were bound—

> ' Such vows, as is a shame
> A man should not be bound by, yet the which
> No man can keep.'

> ' My knights are sworn to vows
> Of utter hardihood, utter gentleness,
> And, loving, utter faithfulness in love,
> And uttermost obedience to the King.'

In the quest won by Gareth against Castle Perilous there
can be traced a symbolic fore-shadowing of the story yet to
come.

Enid shows the first symptoms of doubt and disturbance
spreading from one to another, sprung from the rumour of
the Queen's fatal disloyalty. Trust is not yet destroyed
beyond remedy; the purity of Enid, the faith of Arthur,
restore faith to Geraint.

It is a little hard to understand why Vivien with her sin-
stamped wiles should come in at this stage; she seems to
belong more truly to the later times of shameless outbreak.
Her undisguised wickedness seems to witness to more than

> ' the little rift within the lute,
> That by and by will make the music mute,
> And ever widening slowly silence all.'

Elaine, in exquisitely beautiful fashion, draws the contrast
between her pure love for Lancelot, which he cannot return
because

> ' His honour rooted in dishonour stood,
> And faith unfaithful kept him falsely true ; '

and the unholy passion of Lancelot and Guinevere still hidden from the knowledge of Arthur, and undreamt of by his trusting heart.

Nothing in the whole poem, I think, is more striking than the King's reception of the news concerning the vision of the Holy Grail and the quest in search of it hastily embraced by his knights. To them it seemed a call from highest heaven ; Arthur, clearer-sighted than they, sees in it the neglect of a certain and immediate duty for one at best doubtful, and discerns a presage of coming disaster to the Round Table. The difference is due not to feebler imagination, but to saner judgment. To the great King whose coming and passing are alike veiled in mystery, whose blameless soul is ever in communion with things unseen, to him more than any of them come 'visions of the night or of the day'—

> 'Many a time they come,
> Until this earth he walks on seems not earth,
> This light that strikes his eyeball is not light,
> This air that smites his forehead is not air
> But vision—yea, his very hand and foot—
> In moments when he feels he cannot die,
> And knows himself no vision to himself,
> Nor the high God a vision, nor that One
> Who rose again.'

But he will allow no vision to absorb his mind or turn him aside from the humbler duties laid upon him. Had he been present, his knights assert, he too would have sworn the vow to seek the Holy Grail. 'Not easily,' the King replies,

> 'Not easily, seeing that the King must guard
> That which he rules, and is but as the hind
> To whom a space of land is given to plow.
> Who may not wander from the allotted field
> Before his work be done.'

Having sworn, the knights must go ; but it is with a heavy
heart that Arthur sees the older vow—

> ' To break the heathen and uphold the Christ,
>   To ride abroad redressing human wrongs,'

suspended for the new quest. And when the 'year of
miracle' is over, and the fevered adventures past, when
the thinned ranks gather once more about the King to tell
of Sir Percivale's mirage-visions 'in a land of sand and
thorns,' of days when Sir Bors lay bound and dungeoned,
of Lancelot's maddened ride ; it is only to prove how true
were his forebodings. Most have failed ; many are lost—
' scarce returned a tithe '—and of the few to whom the
vision came,

> ' My greatest hardly will believe he saw ;
>   Another hath beheld it afar off,
>   And leaving human wrongs to right themselves,
>   Cares but to pass into the silent life.
>   And one hath had the vision face to face,
>   And now his chair desires him here in vain,
>   However they may crown him otherwhere.'

The next two idylls, *Pelleas and Ettarre* and *The Last
Tournament*, are painful reading. The new knights made
'to fill the gap left by the Holy Quest' are not like the
old ; the sin of Lancelot and Guinevere has done its fatal
work, and in gloom and treachery and disillusion Arthur's
realm

> ' Reels back into the beast, and is no more.'

Pelleas and Ettarre is unrelieved by any light of Arthur's
presence, or of loyal act; *The Last Tournament*, though

> ' In the heart of Arthur pain was lord,'

has one touch of relief in the faithfulness of Dagonet, the fool, even to the bitter close.

> 'That night came Arthur home, and while he climb'd,
>   All in a death-dumb, autumn-dripping gloom,
>   The stairway to the hall, and look'd and saw
>   The great Queen's bower was dark,—about his feet
>   A voice clung sobbing till he question'd it,
>   "What art thou?" and the voice about his feet
>   Sent up an answer, sobbing, "I am thy fool,
>   And I shall never make thee smile again."'

With *Guinevere* the poem again rises to its highest level. The Queen's agonised self-abasement in 'the holy house at Almesbury,' her too tardy repentance and bitterly remorseful shame, the utter conquest of her love, which Arthur at last achieves in the very crisis of his defeat, attest the King's greatness, and the grandeur of his aims, no less eloquently than his own patience and dignity and self-mastery in the throes of love wounded to the quick, ideals desecrated, purposes destroyed at the hands of his own familiar friends.

> 'We needs must love the highest when we see it,
>   Not Lancelot nor another.'

Guinevere's eyes had remained strangely, perversely blind; she sees now, and it is enough.

Once more in the *Passing of Arthur* Lord Tennyson's power of surrounding persons and events with an atmosphere of dim, unearthly mystery, in lines of haunting beauty, is at its highest. There is a shiver of nameless apprehension in the dream-visit to Arthur of Gawain's ghost, 'blown along a wandering wind,' before 'that last weird battle in the west,' and again in the sense of unreality that clings about the King like the grey mist—

> ' This blind haze, which ever since I saw
> One lying in the dust at Almesbury,
> Hath folded in the passes of the world.'

The battle itself looms phantom-like out of haze—

> ' On the waste sand by the waste sea they closed.
> Nor ever yet had Arthur fought a fight
> Like this last, dim, weird battle of the west.
> A deathwhite mist slept over sand and sea :
> Whereof the chill, to him who breathed it, drew
> Down with his blood, till all his heart was cold
> With formless fear ; and ev'n on Arthur fell
> Confusion, since he saw not whom he fought.'

Before the battle Arthur's steadfast though bewildered trust
makes itself felt through all his grief—

> ' I found Him in the shining of the stars,
> I mark'd Him in the flowering of His fields,
> But in His ways with men I find Him not.
>
> *   *   *   *   *
>
> ' *Perchance, because we see not to the close ;*—
> For I, being simple, thought to work His will,
> And have but stricken with the sword in vain.'

And, again, when all is over, the day lost, the knighthood
scattered for ever, the King himself struck down, laid 'like
a shattered column,' he utters once more the same words
with which in joy and hopefulness he had entered into his
kingdom—

> ' The old order changeth, yielding place to new.'

His trust is vindicated ; Leodogran's dream is fulfilled ; for
through the gates of earthly defeat lies the path to spiritual
victory.   Though the realm has disappeared, the King
himself stands forth still crowned, his courage, his purity,
his truth and faith as much the worship of the new order

as of the old.   Like the old Greek heroes taken up at last
to reign amongst the constellations, the ideal King passes
from the scene of his ruined purpose to shine with brighter
glory in the heaven of spiritual imagination as the stars for
ever and ever.

II.

ROBERT BROWNING.

'This world's no blot for us
Nor blank ; it means intensely and means good :
To find its meaning is my meat and drink.'

Fra Lippo Lippi.

'A man's reach should exceed his grasp,
Or what's a heaven for ? '—*Andrea del Sarto.*

THERE is still a curiously sharp line of cleavage between
people who read and treasure the poetry of Browning,
and people who are deterred from attempting it by a
fixed impression that he is unintelligible.   At one extreme
he is treated with the deference paid to an oracle—though
never since Shakespeare, one would think, could there have
been poetry lending itself less naturally to the purposes of
an exclusive 'cult' ;—while the other extreme wraps itself
in a mantle of comfortable contempt for an unread author,
partly perhaps in protest against over-adoration of him ;
for Browning, like Wordsworth, has suffered a little at the
hands of his friends.   Between the two extremes are many
who read, and learn, and enjoy quietly and keenly ;
and many more who would share to the full in the
enjoyment and learning if they once began the reading.

The obscurity in Browning's style is the obstacle alleged.
But there has been much exaggeration on this score.   Leaving
aside some of the early, and a considerable part of his

latest, work, there remains a great body of poetry which is hardly ever obscure. This is not the same thing as saying that it is not *difficult;* most of it is difficult to some extent; some of it is very difficult; that is, it needs close and undivided attention before it can be followed with clear understanding. Often the thought is intricate; its turns sudden and abrupt; but while needless obscurity might lead us to suspect that mental poverty was disguised in it, and excuse us from the pains of unveiling it, difficulty surely offers no reason why we should forego that which abundantly repays the exertion it costs. Nor need any one, through inability or disinclination to grapple with the whole of works so voluminous as to have been called 'not a book but a literature,' be denied the delight of acquaintance with the many poems that a very moderate effort cannot but render intelligible to ordinary intelligence.

It seems very possible that Browning's rugged, abbreviated style is intentionally adopted in order to rouse the attention (so easily lulled by well-accustomed forms) that his meaning demands; at any rate it is plain that he can produce smooth verse and melody when he chooses. Take *The Lost Leader*, for example—

> ' We that had loved him so, followed him, honoured him,
> Lived in his mild and magnificent eye,
> Learned his great language, caught his clear accents,
> Made him our pattern to live and to die ! '

Or the *Cavalier Tunes*, or this quietly musical stanza from *Two in the Campagna*—

> ' The champaign with its endless fleece
> Of feathery grasses everywhere :
> Silence and passion, joy and peace,
> An everlasting wash of air—
> Rome's ghost since her decease.'

Or the whole of the lovely poem on Guercino's picture of *The Guardian Angel*, especially, perhaps, these two stanzas—

> ' Dear and great Angel, wouldst thou only leave,
>   That child, when thou hast done with him, for me !
> Let me sit all the day here, that when eve
>   Shall find performed thy special ministry,
> And time come for departure, thou, suspending
> Thy flight, may'st see another child for tending,
>   Another still to quiet and retrieve.
>
> *   *   *   *
>
> ' If this were ever granted, I would rest
>   My head beneath thine, while thy healing hands
> Close covered both my eyes beside thy breast,
>   Pressing the brain which too much thought expands,
> Back to its proper size again, and smoothing
> Distortion down till every nerve had soothing,
>   And all lay quiet, happy and suppressed.'

Or once more this, of the bust of the infant emperor Protus—

> ' One loves a baby face, with violets there,
>   Violets instead of laurel in the hair,
>   As those were all the little locks could bear.'

Nor do these by any means stand alone. But neither do they in the least represent the style Browning commonly uses, a vigorous, terse, sometimes crabbed and eccentric style, in which a word often stands for a sentence, parentheses are rife, and sound is not unfrequently sacrificed to sense. Still, with a little time allowed for becoming accustomed to the unique ways of this mode of expression, the moderate effort aforesaid renders a large number of these poems not only intelligible but intensely attractive.

Their great attractive power lies in the sense for the sake of which beauty in form gives way; for they are the out-

come of a mind whose vivifying imagination combined with
a searching power of analysis, shows as only a great poet
can, the hidden significance he finds in our common human
life; and both what he sees and the interpretation he puts
upon it are saturated with living interest. Some of us may
be fortunate enough to count among our friends one whose
way of viewing things makes commonplace events interesting and rare ones positively thrilling, one to whom we
always care to tell even trivial experiences for the sake of
the illuminating word that is sure to come in reply. It is
said of the late Dr. John Brown, of Edinburgh—' "I'll tell
Dr. Brown," was the thought that came first to his friends
on hearing anything genuine, pathetic, or queer, and the
gleam as of sunlight that shone in his eyes, and played
round his sensitive mouth as he listened, acted as an
inspiration, so that friends and even strangers he saw at
their best, and their best was better than it would have been
without him.' So is Mr. Browning among the poets. Not
that we can take our experiences to him; but that is
needless; he is already amply provided, and, unasked, will
give *us* of his best.

He cares before all things for individual human life.
Not for the life of nations and races, or the movements of
political parties or social classes, but for the life-story of
Filippo or Jacynth, Smith and Kate; and nothing about
them escapes or fails to interest him, from the inmost
recesses of Filippo's thoughts to the way Kate does her hair.
That is the first thing. Next, he brings these men and
women thronging before us; they are *there*, living and real,
with faults, virtues, joys, griefs, in strength or in weakness,
like the men and women we know in our every-day lives, or
rather *should* know if we had heart and insight enough to

read them as we are shown these. Sometimes indeed the determination to 'make speak '—

'The very man as he was wont to do—'

leads to total disregard of the canon that requires art to be beautiful as well as true, as in the positive ugliness of the first part of *Holy Cross Day;* but this is an extreme case. Lastly, through the treatment of these actual men and women, most of them not in the least ideal people, some of them as queerly grotesque as one can well imagine, we arrive at the poet's own ideal of life, and find an ideal not only interesting, but in the highest degree stimulating, inspiring, bracing. For in a way, Browning is after all the soul of all his creations. They speak, but we feel that he, the observer, is there all the time, and somehow through their own speech we discern his judgment of them; out of his own mouth is

'Announced to each his station in the Past,—'

not, of course, as the world judges, but according as they stand in the poet's view of life.

It is therefore all-important to understand what this view of life, broadly speaking, is. Browning clearly regards this life as a preparation for 'more life and fuller' beyond the veil; a time which, to be spent rightly, must be spent in growth, progress, a constant rising from lower to higher things through a never-ending series of experiences that discipline, be they joys or pains. He delights in the joys of life not as ends, but means; he greets the pains of life not as evils, but as further means, the cause of struggle indeed, but of health-giving struggle, without which we should be the losers.

> ' Then, welcome each rebuff
> That turns earth's smoothness rough,
> Each sting that bids nor sit nor stand but go !
> Be our joys three-parts pain !
> Strive, and hold cheap the strain ;
> Learn, nor account the pang ; dare, never grudge the throe.
>
> *Rabbi Ben Ezra.*

He does not place his ideal in disciplined obedience to law and duty, but in disciplined *activity*, continuous aspiration from height to height.

> ' I say that man was made to grow, not stop ;
> That help, he needed once, and needs no more,
> Having grown but an inch by, is withdrawn :
> For he hath new needs, and new helps to these.
> This imports solely, man should mount on each
> New height in view.'

*   *   *   *   *

> ' Man knows partly but conceives beside,
> Creeps ever on from fancies to the fact,
> And in this striving, this converting air
> Into a solid he may grasp and use,
> Finds progress, man's distinctive mark alone,
> Not God's, and not the beasts' : God is, they are,
> Man partly is and wholly hopes to be.'
>
> *A Death in the Desert.*

Steady growth from less to more perfect knowledge ; to stronger, because more reasonable, steadfastness of will ; to finer spiritual insight—the eye ever quicker to perceive the occasional 'God-glimpse,' the ear to catch the 'first low word' of divine incitement ; this carried on from youth to age he regards as the true life to be lived here, the true preparation for 'the last of life for which the first was made.'

> ' And I shall thereupon
> Take rest ere I be gone
> Once more on my adventure brave and new :
> Fearless and unperplexed,
> When I wage battle next,
> What weapons to select, what armour to indue.'
>
> *Rabbi Ben Ezra.*

It follows that progress of this kind must be accompanied by a frequent consciousness of failure as the man's reach still exceeds his grasp, and the goal of aspiration is attained only to prove itself unsatisfying. Browning's doctrine of defeat might be summed up in weighty words written by a well-known teacher with a very different application. 'To be defeated,' says the late Mr. Edward Thring, 'and go on the better for being defeated, is the highest thing that can happen to man. There is no blessing equal to defeat. . . . Defeat is the hallowed means by which greatness is made great.'

'For thence,' says Rabbi Ben Ezra—

> ' For thence,—a paradox
> Which comforts while it mocks,—
> Shall life succeed in that it seems to fail :
> What I aspired to be,
> And was not, comforts me :
> A brute I might have been, but would not sink i' the scale.'

And again in *The Grammarian's Funeral* Browning's view is emphasised—

> ' That low man seeks a little thing to do,
>   Sees it and does it :
> This high man, with a great thing to pursue,
>   Dies ere he knows it.
> That low man goes on adding one to one,
>   His hundred's soon hit :
> This high man, aiming at a million,
>   Misses an unit.

> That has the world here—should he need the next,
>   Let the world mind him !
> This, throws himself on God, and unperplexed,
>   Seeking shall find him.'

There are two opposite snares to be avoided by him who would live truly. One is forgetfulness of the conditions of this present life, the limitations which forbid a premature attempt to force infinite achievement into the finite existence, to gain perfect knowledge, unbounded exercise of will, undimmed perception, limitless emotion, to crowd the work of eternity into the brief years of time. That way lies destruction to the spirit. The other snare is acquiescence in ordinary standards, contentment with easily-won things of earthly life, of which the best is nothing—

> ' Unless we turn, as the soul knows how,
>   The earthly gift to an end divine.'

Browning has absolutely no patience at all with apathy and feebleness.

> ' What had I on earth to do,
>   With the slothful, with the mawkish, the unmanly ?
> Like the aimless, helpless, hopeless did I drivel ? '
>
> > Epilogue to *Asolando*.

He denounces the man or woman who stifles an arousing impulse in obedience to prudential motives,—this seems clearly to be the bearing of *The Statue and the Bust*, which has strangely enough been construed into an approval of license.

> ' He looked at her, as a lover can ;
>   She looked at him as one who awakes :
> The past was a sleep, and her life began.'

Their love was unlawful, but not for this reason did they refuse to indulge it. No sense of duty restrained them,

nothing more exalted than sloth and cowardice ; they clung
to the unfaithful love—the 'counter'—yet hung back from
venturing aught for it, and therefore

> ' The counter, our lovers staked, was lost
> As surely as if it were lawful coin :
>
> And the sin I impute to each frustrate ghost
> Is, the unlit lamp and the ungirt loin,
> Through the end in sight was a vice, I say.'

In *Easter Day* the soul which longed for nothing more
than earth can give receives in a dream-vision the award
of free possession of the world.

> ' Thou art shut
> Out of the heaven of spirit ; glut
> Thy sense upon the world : 'tis thine
> For ever—take it ! '

But the transport of joy that the award at first occasions
is changed by degrees into dark despair as the soul realises
too late what it is to have accepted for eternity the limitations of earth ; and the beseeching prayer breaks out—

> ' Thou Love of God ! Or let me die,
> Or grant what shall seem heaven almost !
> Let me not know that all is lost,
> Though lost it be—leave me not tied
> To this despair, this corpse-like bride !
> Let that old life seem mine—no more—
> With limitation as before,
> With darkness, hunger, toil, distress :
> Be all the earth a wilderness !
> Only let me go on, go on,
> Still hoping ever and anon
> To reach one eve the Better Land ! '

And when the dread vision is gone by, the lesson of
strenuous living has been effectually learnt.

> And so I live, you see,
> Go through the world, try, prove, reject,
> Prefer, still struggling to effect
> My warfare; happy that I can
> Be crossed and thwarted as a man,
> Not left in God's contempt apart,
> With ghastly smooth life, dead at heart,
> Tame in earth's paddock as her prize.'

The connoisseur also, he whose attitude is merely that of appraising, however accurately, the products of Art, fares even worse at Mr. Browning's hands than at Lord Tennyson's. The builder of the Palace of Art is saved at last; but for the Bishop who orders his tomb at St. Praxed's what prospect is there? His unexceptionable taste in the matter of marble, *lapis lazuli*, bronze work, inscriptions—

> 'Carve my epitaph aright,
> Choice Latin, picked phrase, Tully's every word,
> No gaudy ware like Gandolf's second line—
> Tully my masters? Ulpian serves his need!'

—ministers to nothing higher than vanity, spite, distrust, cynical worldliness, curiously blended with a genuine regard for customary ritual, a relish for 'good, strong, thick, stupefying incense-smoke'; his whole conception of Art, as a mere means of self-exaltation, seeming the more degraded under the reverend episcopal cope and mitre.

Contrast with this, *Abt Vogler*, the genuine artist, 'made perfect' for a moment with the wonderful palace of music reared

> All through my keys that gave their sounds to a wish of my soul,
> All through my soul that praised as its wish flowed visibly forth,
> All through music and me!'

As the beautiful sounds die away, and starting tears witness

to their glory and their failure—for they are gone—he lifts
the more surely arms of aspiration to the God in whom all
fulness shall be found without change.

'Therefore to whom turn I but to thee, the ineffable Name?
  Builder and maker, thou, of houses not made with hands!
What, have fear of change from thee who art ever the same?
  Doubt that thy power can fill the heart that thy power expands?
There shall never be one lost good! What was, shall live as before;
  The evil is null, is nought, is silence implying sound;
What was good, shall be good, with, for evil, so much good more;
  On the earth the broken arcs; in the heaven, a perfect round.
    *   *   *   *   *   *
And what is our failure here but a triumph's evidence
  For the fulness of the days?'

This is the apotheosis of noble failure; but even for
ignoble and seemingly absolute failure Browning, always
an optimist through his own deeply-grounded confidence
in a governing Intelligence perfect in love as well as in
power, and through his acceptance of evil as a necessary
condition of good in this school of the soul, has something
hopeful to say. Musing in the Morgue over such an
unpromising text as the sight of

'The three men who did most abhor
Their life in Paris yesterday,
  So killed themselves:'

he concludes—

'My own hope is, a sun will pierce
The thickest cloud earth ever stretched;
  That, after Last, returns the First,
Though a wide compass round be fetched;
  That what began best, can't end worst,
Nor what God blessed once, prove accurst.'
                              Apparent Failure.

Browning is the sympathetic exponent of all sorts of

incident, of every kind of enthusiastic activity, in this life-long growth of the single soul. Bodily development, music, painting, poetry, love, hate, patriotism, hero-worship, the life of cities and towns, country life, theology, philosophy—hardly any imaginable human interest bearing on it lies outside his range of interest. Only a few of the most important can be touched upon here.

He sets high value on the body, and the happy, efficient exercise of all its faculties—

> ' Oh, our manhood's prime vigour ! No spirit feels waste,
> Not a muscle is stopped in its playing nor sinew unbraced.
> Oh ! the wild joys of living ! the leaping from rock up to rock,
> The strong rending of boughs from the fir-tree, the cool silver shock
> Of the plunge in a pool's living water.'—*Saul*.

It is recognised, too, as a most precious instrument—

> ' Eyes, ears took in their dole,
> Brain treasured up the whole,
> Should not the heart beat once "How good to live and learn ?"'

And again—

> ' Let us not always say
> " Spite of this flesh to-day
> I strove, made head, gained ground upon the whole !"
> As the bird wings and sings,
> Let us cry " All good things
> Are ours, nor soul helps flesh more, now, than flesh helps soul !"'
> *Rabbi Ben Ezra.*

Browning is so pre-occupied with man, or rather men, that nature, except in its bearing on the mood or life of some human being here and there, has a comparatively small share in his poetry. But amongst his crowded gallery of characters some are keenly susceptible to the influence of skies, hills, and flowers ; and from them we get descriptive

passages of great and original beauty. These touch oftenest
upon the larger aspects of nature, such as impress the
beholder with their revelation of power and majesty. Sometimes the picture is subdued in tone, as in the stanza quoted
before from *Two in the Campagna;* sometimes a lovely detail
is brought out,—

> ' That's the wise thrush : he sings each song twice over
> Lest you should think he never could recapture
> The first fine careless rapture ! '
> > *Home Thoughts from Abroad.*

Sometimes details are richly multiplied, as in *The English-
man in Italy*, but oftener the tone of grandeur prevails, as
when the Grammarian's lofty burial-place is described—

> ' Here—here's his place, where meteors shoot, clouds form,
> Lightnings are loosened,
> Stars come and go ! Let joy break with the storm,
> Peace let the dew send ! '

The speaker in *Christmas Eve* bears emphatic testimony
to the constraining impulse of worship found by some so
much more powerful under the solemn, lonely sky than in
any narrower shrine. He has burst out of Zion Chapel,
oppressed by

> ' the pig-of-lead-like pressure
> Of the preaching man's immense stupidity,'

into the fresh, dark, storm-swept night. He describes a lull
in the rain and wind, the piled-up clouds, the flying moon,
the shifting tints of halo. With lightened brain he grows
calmer, and tolerance returns, but the ways of other men
will never be his, though his attitude towards them has yet
to be greatly modified.

> ' Oh, let men keep their ways
> Of seeking thee in a narrow shrine—
> Be this my way !   And this is mine ! '

Immediately afterwards, in the sudden light of 'the moon's consummate apparition,' there springs up before him a sight described in a passage palpitating with breathless wonder and expectation—

> ' North and South and East lay ready
> For a glorious thing that, dauntless, deathless,
>   Sprang across them and stood steady.
> 'Twas a moon-rainbow, vast and perfect,
> From heaven to heaven extending, perfect
> As the mother-moon's self, full in face.
> It rose, distinctly at the base
>   With its seven proper colours chorded,
> Which still, in the rising, were compressed,
> Until at last they coalesced,
>   And supreme the spectral creature lorded
> In a triumph of whitest white,
> Above which intervened the night.
> But above night too, like only the next,
>   The second of a wondrous sequence,
>   Reaching in rare and rarer fragrance,
> Till the heaven of heavens were circumflexed,
> Another rainbow rose, a mightier,
> Fainter, flushier and flightier,
> Rapture dying along its verge.
> Oh, whose foot shall I see emerge,
> Whose, from the straining topmost dark,
> On to the keystone of that arc ? '

In *Pippa Passes* another radiant passage tells how Luigi, in prospect of death, will carry word to all in the other world who care to hear of sunshine and storm, dying days and moonlit nights.

> ' God must be glad one loves his world so much.
>   I can give news of earth to all the dead
>   Who ask me :—last year's sunsets, and great stars
>   Which had a right to come first and see ebb,
>   The crimson wave that drifts the sun away—

> Those crescent moons with notched and burning rims
> That strengthened into sharp fire, and these stood,
> Impatient of the azure—and that day
> In March, a double rainbow stopped the storm—
> May's warm slow yellow moonlit summer nights—
> Gone are they, but I have them in my soul ! '

To pass to another subject, no other poet has attempted, as Browning does, to trace out in words the charm and mystery of musical sounds. The grandest of these poems, *Abt Vogler*, has already been mentioned ; it shows not only delight in harmonised tones, but learned and minute know-ledge of musical theory. Then there is the delightful *Toccata of Galuppi's*, with its bright yet half ironical and half melancholy picture of Venetian life ; and *Master Hugues of Saxe Gotha*, in which the organist, left by himself in the dim church, demands of the great dead composer whose music has just taxed his fingers and filled his soul with excitement,

> ' What do you mean by your mountainous fugues ? '

How vividly the somewhat eerie details of the time and place are brought out,—the church left to its darkness and silence, the glimmer of light from the burning scrap of candle in the organ-loft, the deep shades among the forest of organ-pipes, where, as the organist plays, the master's face seems to lurk—

> ' . . . with brow ruled like a score
> Yes, and eyes buried in 'pits on each cheek,
>   Like two great breves as they wrote them of yore,
> Each side that bar, your straight beak ! '

Here again it takes some technical knowledge of music to understand fully the masterly merits of the fugue-descrip-tion that follows ; and then what are we to make of the unfinished comparison at the end, the misgivings that *will* force their way through the prevailing belief that the greater mind knows best, lest all the labour is after all a mere darkening of counsel as the spreading spider-webs overhead blot out the golden roof? We are left to think it out for ourselves; and meantime what dramatic force there is in the abrupt end,—the player's irritable nerves suddenly and badly upset, and his philosophising cut short by the sputter of dying candle.

> '. . . Lo you the wick in the socket !
> Hallo, you sacristan, show us a light there !
>   Down it dips, gone like a rocket.
> What, you want, do you, to come unawares,
> Sweeping the church up for first morning prayers,
> And find a poor devil has ended his cares
> At the foot of your rotten-runged rat-riddled stairs ?
>   Do I carry the moon in my pocket ? '

Independently of the poems actually devoted to music, many a passing phrase or allusion shows Browning's quick ear for it—

> ' We shall have the word
>   In a minor third,
> There is none but the cuckoo knows.'

No less characteristic are his poems on pictures and painting. In the course of the thoughts they contain about Art, its truth, its falsehood, its ideal of excellence, its office in quickening men's perceptions, or lifting up their thoughts, his own view of life and method of communicating it receive vivid illustration.

> 'For, don't you mark? we're so made that we love
> First when we see them painted, things we have passed
> Perhaps a hundred times nor cared to see ;
> And so they are better painted—better to us,
> Which is the same thing. Art was given for that ;

> God uses us to help each other so,
> Lending our minds out.　Have you noticed, now
> Your cullion's hanging face?　A bit of chalk
> And trust me but you should, though !　How much more
> If I drew higher things with the same truth !
> That were to take the Prior's pulpit place,
> Interpret God to all of you.'

So *Fra Lippo Lippi* says, himself a marked example of
Browning's courage in acceptance of the amazing incongrui-
ties of human life.　Here is Brother Lippo with the artist-soul
of a lover of the beautiful in the body of a rollicking monk,
caught in the very act of a disreputable escapade, and
lavishing excuses and clever blandishments upon his captors
along with his heavenly theories of Art.

Andrea del Sarto (called 'The faultless painter') shows
that the absence of defects cannot compensate for the
absence of genius.　With all his faultless technical skill, the
painter sees himself below the least of the inspired painters
whose reach exceeds their grasp—craftsman not artist, he
calls himself.　All that his mind can conceive his hand can
execute—

> 'Easily, too—when I say, perfectly,
> I do not boast, perhaps.'

His drawing and colouring are flawless—but the *meaning?*

> 'All the play, the insight and the stretch—
> Out of me, out of me !'

Rafael's drawing may be wrong, but the light of heaven
shines through the faulty lines, 'its soul is right.'　Had but
Andrea's beautiful wife been able to supply the inspiration
he needed, he too might have risen at her word with Agnolo
and Rafael, 'up to God all three'; but the two objects of
his divided passion, his Art and his cold-hearted, shallow-

brained wife, are alike, perfect in physical loveliness but lacking soul. And so he acquiesces sadly in the small return his devotion to either can secure.

Old Pictures in Florence draws the same contrast between outward skill and the expression of inward meaning in another way. Here the ancient art of Greece is compared with the pictures of the early Christian painters; the perfection of visible lineament and stature in the one is set against the struggling spiritual significance of the other.

> 'On which I conclude, that the early painters
>   To cries of "Greek Art and what more wish you?"—
> Replied, "To become now self-acquainters,
>   And paint man, man, whatever the issue!
> Make new hopes shine through the flesh they fray,
>   New fears aggrandize the rags and tatters:
> To bring the invisible into full play,
>   Let the visible go to the dogs—what matters?"'

Passing on to the heaped-up riches of the love-poems we again find that Browning's general view of life determines and explains his attitude; and looking at them as far as possible from the same point of view, even more clearly than before we

> 'Discern
> Infinite passion, and the pain
> Of finite hearts that yearn.'

For he regards love as one of the best, or perhaps *the* best and most powerful means of enlightenment among the whole series of enlightening experiences in which the value of life makes itself felt. Genuine love even more surely than art or learning renovates the soul and widens its horizon. Moreover, it is the commonest; anybody *may* have it—it is 'a thing men seldom miss.'

> ' God be thanked, the meanest of his creatures
>   Boasts two soul-sides, one to face the world with,
>   One to show a woman when he loves her ! '

To reject it through fear or prudence or inertness is to be
tried in the balances and found wanting, and to forego
life's best gift. And this is true for men and women
equally, for Browning is in direct opposition to the common
notion which thinks of love as the main part of a woman's
life, but only an episode in a man's.

His work here is quite new in the degree to which the
lovers are *real*, not idealised people; just men and women,
passionate or cold, true or faithless, as in actual life.
Also he goes far beyond the early rapture to which most
other love-poetry is confined, and follows out the results
in after-days, when some barrier may have kept the lovers
asunder, or when, after marriage, love has declined through
miserable stages of decay, or union has grown ever closer
and dearer. No two situations are alike in these varied
poems, of pure love-rapture; of love checked by timidity
or prudence, made tragic by caprice, frustrated by circumstances, cut short by death; of love turned delirious; of
love perfect on one side and faulty on the other; above all,
of ideal love crowned in perfect union.

To come to individual poems. Simple passion animates
Meeting at Night—

> ' A voice less loud, through joys and fears
>   Than the two hearts beating each to each ; '

and the daring *Confessions*—

> ' We loved, sir—used to meet :
>   How sad and bad and mad it was—
>   But then, how it was sweet ! '

In *Dis Aliter Visum* an old French *savant* has fallen in
love with a young beauty 'round and sound as a mountain
apple'; his love is returned, but his prudence forbids the
marriage—for them there was to be

> 'No grasping at love, gaining a share
>   O' the sole spark from God's life at strife
> With death.'

Ten years later they meet again; he has married a dancer,
she a man she does not care for, and so she tells her lover
his worldly-wise cowardice has lost 'two souls; nay four.'

In *Youth and Art* the two have missed the mutual love
that might have been theirs, and so though one has married
a lord, and the other has gained his ambition and ranks
high as an artist—

> 'Each life's unfulfilled, you see;
>   It hangs still, patchy and scrappy;
> We have not sighed deep, laughed free,
>   Starved, feasted, despaired,—been happy.'

The last two lines strike a vein in which Browning is
supremely successful, as he depicts the keen enjoyment that
two congenial souls get out of companionship in all and
any circumstances, no matter how trivial or disagreeable to
outside eyes.   Glance at the snowed-up couple in *A Lovers'
Quarrel*—

> 'Laughs with so little cause !
> We devised games out of straws.
>   We would try and trace
>   One another's face
> In the ash, as an artist draws ;
>   Free on each other's flaws,
> How we chattered like two church daws ! '

And in *Respectability*, how happy they are to have escaped

comfortable, conventional, but separated, life for life together in a back street of Paris.

In *Cristina* she has deliberately led him into love and turned away from him. Which is the loser? and what has the other gained?

> 'Such am I : the secret's mine now! She has lost me, I have gained
> her ;
> Her soul's mine : and thus, grown perfect, I shall pass my life's
> remainder.
> Life will just hold out the proving both our powers, alone and
> blended :
> And then, come next life quickly! This world's use will have been
> ended.'

He has 'caught God's secret,' separation cannot deprive him of it ; it is her life that is left imperfect. '*She has lost me, I have gained her.*'

In *Too Late* she has married the wrong man, and after six years is dead ; and his (the right man's) anguish breaks out, and his contempt for 'that blank lay-figure your fancy draped '—

> 'See, I bleed these tears in the dark
> Till comfort come and the last be bled :
> He? He is tagging your epitaph.'

And the heart-break sobs through commonplace words of almost playful remembrance.

The passionate lovers of *In a Gondola* are parted by the hand of the assassin, whose stab is hardly suffered to interrupt their speech before it is stilled in death. *Porphyria's* lover himself calls death to his aid to free his beloved from the 'vainer ties' she could not escape in life. This poem was originally among those purporting to have been written from *Madhouse Cells*.

In *The Worst of It* the marriage has failed; she has proved faithless, and his loyal, unselfish heart grieves first that *she*, his pride and joy, should be touched by the finger of desecration; next that his very devotion must some day be the knife for her stabbing; and worst of all, that even should she now repent it would be for her own sake, not for his or love's, and so for a heaven at best but a place of cold glitter and shine. The deed is done, their fate sealed; and for all his unquenched love he ends with the irrevocable sentence—

> 'I knew you once : but in Paradise
> If we meet, I will pass nor turn my head.'

In *Any Wife to Any Husband* she, the deeper nature of the two, is dying before he is perfected in love as he might and would have been could she have remained at his side.

> 'And is it not the bitterer to think
> That, disengage our hands and thou wilt sink
> Although thy love was love in very deed ? '

In *A Forgiveness*, before the terrible interruption to love occurs, there is a matchless ideal of the inspiring effect of love on daily work—

> ' Work freely done should balance happiness
> Fully enjoyed ; and since beneath my roof
> Housed she who made home heaven, in heaven's behoof
> I went forth every day, and all day long
> Worked for the world.'

Lastly, there are the poems of flawless love and life. Their proportion—two only, out of a number of which barely the fourth part has had even a word here—speaks its own tale.

By the Fireside brings us into the inner heaven of home itself, where love and union reign secure. Years of love ever ripening and deepening have made of them 'one soul,' and now he watches her as she sits

> 'Reading by fire-light, that great brow
> And the spirit small hand propping it,
> Mutely, my heart knows how—
>
> 'When, if I think but deep enough,
> You are wont to answer, prompt as rhyme ;
> And you, too, find without rebuff
> Response your soul seeks many a time,
> Piercing its fine flesh-stuff.'

He goes back in thought to the moment among the wood-land trees that took away the screen of division from between them.

> 'How the world is made for each of us !
> How all we perceive and know in it
> Tends to some moment's product thus,
> When a soul declares itself—to wit
> By its fruit, the thing it does.
> 　　*　　　*　　　*　　　*　　　*
> 'I am named and known by that moment's feat ;
> There took my station and degree ;
> So grew my own small life complete,
> As Nature obtained her best of me—
> One born to love you, sweet !
> 　　*　　　*　　　*　　　*　　　*
> 'So, earth has gained by one man the more,
> And the gain of earth must be heaven's gain too.'

In *One Word More*, the dedication of his *Men and Women*, the poet speaks 'once, and only once, and for one only' in his own name to his own wife.

Another remarkable class of poems is concerned either with subtle dissection of characters such as men endure but do not praise, or with investigation of some belief or philosophy. In *Caliban, Mr. Sludge the Medium, Bishop Blougram*, Mr. Browning allows abject ignorance and super- stition, prejudice, cunning, ecclesiastical sophistry and worldly wisdom, to say their best for themselves, and in the saying to display themselves unveiled. Whether the result is regarded as merely a dramatic presentation marked by extraordinary skill and insight, or as also a castigating satire, will depend on the reader's point of view.

All these poems are difficult, and need most careful reading and re-reading; but it would be hard to say which best repays the study it demands, so keen an interest can each one of them arouse. In *Cleon*, the Greek poet, re- plying to questions from Protus, the Emperor, passes from stage to stage of a subtle argument involving some of the most difficult problems of life, till he arrives at a point from which it appears that the only possible solution for the crown- ing perplexity lies in the promise of a future life. But at this point the poet-philosopher is turned back upon himself, for

> 'Zeus has not yet revealed it; and alas,
> He must have done so were it possible.'

By a most characteristic touch Cleon's letter is ended with a contemptuous allusion to 'one called Paulus,' who at that moment was delivering the message of revelation that Cleon longs for with his whole soul. He reproaches the Emperor for stopping to inquire of such an one—

> 'He writeth, doth he? Well, and he may write.'

The Jew finds his proper scholars in 'certain slaves' who preach him and Christ—

> 'And (as I gathered from a bystander)
> Their doctrine could be held by no sane man.'

The cultivated Greek can by no means bring himself even to hear the words of a barbarian Jew.

An Epistle works out a still more intricate problem. It endeavours to realise in imagination the effect upon a man's life here of having actually experienced the life of another world, from which he has returned to earth; and it conveys this to the reader, not directly, but through the impression which such a case may be supposed to have made upon the mind of a beholder—in this case Karshish, the Arab physician, a man trained by his occupation to observe and reason, and familiar with the symptoms of mental aberration or bodily disease. The double effort of imagination involved complicates the problem, but adds greatly to its dramatic force and interest. Karshish, travelling in India, writes to the master-sage Abib, his instructor, and after passing lightly in review certain ailments and remedies he has found common in the land, he enters at length into the 'case' of Lazarus, met with at Bethany, whose epileptic mania is distinguished from common hallucinations by the fact that it remains fixed instead of giving way to time and health. In a state of bodily health far beyond the average, Lazarus is still firmly convinced that, so far from having passed through an ordinary trance, he actually died, and was restored to life 'by a Nazarene physician of his tribe'; and Karshish then tells of the strange paradoxes observable in his conduct. He has seemingly lost all sense of proportion, 'eyes the world now like a child,' is often totally indifferent in the face of great events, and at other moments as unexpectedly indignant or alarmed over some trifle. Yet he is no fool, and Karshish dimly discerns that he has *some* standard by which to judge the importance of earthly matters; he half admits that Lazarus 'knows God's

secret,' and is inclined to admire his 'prone submission to
the heavenly will.' It is left for us to notice that to Lazarus
material concerns have one and all sunk into such utter
insignificance that the conquest of a province is of no more
account than

> ' The passing of a mule with gourds,'

and his child's physical illness gives him scarcely a thought,
while on the other hand, everything touching the moral and
spiritual life has become so supremely important that an
unhallowed look or gesture can throw him into an agony.
But Karshish, while he tries to make light of Lazarus'
'crazy tale,' is in spite of himself fascinated by it, and
cannot maintain an unshaken belief in his own theory of
'mania.' He becomes at last impatient with himself and
apologetic to his master for the undue length of detail into
which he has strayed; but then, after a final farewell, the
indifference in which he would fain take refuge suddenly
breaks down, and he adds after all a few lines of intensely
earnest questioning—

> 'The very God ! think, Abib ; dost thou think ?
> So, the All-Great were the All-Loving too—
> So, through the thunder comes a human voice
> Saying, "O heart I made, a heart beats here !
> Face, My hands fashioned, see it in Myself !
> Thou hast no power nor may'st conceive of mine :
> But love I gave thee, with Myself to love,
> And thou must love Me who have died for thee ! "
> The madman saith He said so : it is strange.'

The revelation of divine love that Karshish incredulously
yet longingly catches at, is again the climax, more clearly
discerned, more firmly held, in *Saul;* but is there arrived
at by a very different process. David, in his efforts to

arouse King Saul out of the trance of misery in which he
hung 'drear and stark, blind and dumb,' plays first the well-
known tunes associated with quiet every-day occupations
of life, and with its sorrows and gladness; then he dwells
on the physical joys of living; then on the delights of such
powers and gifts as Saul possesses, from which he passes
to the more intangible source of happiness to be found in
the thought of Saul's deathless fame. And then, through
the very strength of his own longing—'had love but the
warrant love's heart to dispense '— to restore Saul the
mistake, Saul the failure, the ruin, to new light and life, new
harmony of being,—the truth bursts upon him, and he mocks
at himself for having vainly imagined that he, the creature,
the receiver of gifts, could in the one way of love outdo
the Giver, the Creator. He realises that, as his own perfect
love and service would lead him gladly to take suffering
or death if he could thereby help the king, so it must be
with Him who has the power as well as the will ; and there
breaks upon him with a dizzying shock the assurance that
restoration, completion in a new life *will* be given to Saul,
and this not by a mere fiat, costing nothing, but through
the voluntary suffering and endurance of the One mighty
to save—

> ' So shall crown thee the topmost, ineffablest, uttermost crown—
>   And thy love fill infinitude wholly, nor leave up nor down
>   One spot for the creature to stand in ! '

The Hebrew seer, Rabbi Ben Ezra, also, though his
theology is necessarily Theistic, not Christian, has received
in the purged vision of his old age the same essential truth—

> ' I see the whole design,
>   I, who saw power, see now love perfect too ; '

while in *A Death in the Desert* the aged and last-surviving apostle St. John anticipates the doubts and questionings with which generations to come will assail the gospel he has taught, and answers them with applications of his central doctrine—love and the divinity of love.

> 'For life with all it yields of joy and woe,
> And hope and fear,—believe the aged friend,—
> Is just our chance o' the prize of learning love.'

Indeed we seem here to have come to the very heart of Mr. Browning's own theology. It would of course be both unfair and unsafe to draw any such conclusion only from words put dramatically into the mouth of other speakers; but comparing these with other passages at greater length than is here possible, we may find that he looks upon Christ in a mystical sense as the necessary revelation of divine love, and love as the one indispensable channel of communication between man and God. Through love Omnipotence becomes veritable Divinity; through love man, the creature, shares in the nature of his Creator, and can draw ever closer to Him. It is natural that some expression of belief so fundamental should recur again and again; but one more example must here be enough. It shall be taken from the speaker in *Christmas Eve*.

> '—Love which, on earth, amid all the shows of it,
> Has ever been seen the sole good of life in it,
> The love, ever growing there, spite of the strife in it,
> Shall arise, made perfect, from death's repose of it,
> And I shall behold thee, face to face,
> O God, and in thy light retrace
> How in all I loved here, still wast thou!'

Nearly all illustrations so far have been taken from poems contained in the two volumes of *Selections* made by the poet himself. Almost every quality that is of most value in Mr. Browning's poetry—the insight, the vigour, the exuberant vitality, the keen intellectual interest—is to be found in these dramatic monologues at its best and strongest, and I can only hope that this bare outline, which is all that could be attempted, may suggest enough idea of the wealth of interest to be found in them to lead a few readers as yet unfamiliar with their richness and power and variety, to search further and enjoy for themselves.

Of the dramas it is equally impossible to write with any approach to fulness, but a little must be said, for we would not willingly stop short of them. To some of us it is perhaps in the nature of luxury to go further, but such an irresistible luxury, and we may fairly add, so far from enervating, that only the sternest demands upon time can make us forego it.

The dramas came before the shorter poems in point of time, and they are for the most part less difficult. They are really *plays*, some of them having, as we know, successfully stood the test of actual representation on the stage; yet they are, one would think, better to read than to watch, because in them also the chief interest lies rather in the springs of action than in action itself. The action is commonly indeed quite unimportant, sometimes trivial; *Pippa Passes*, the most charming of all, has the least exciting plot. Then, too, a resemblance in the manner of speech between one and another of the persons speaking—the well-known, abrupt, terse, piquant manner, and the occasional word dropped by one and another of comment that could never have come from the inside of the situation, betray the fact that Mr. Browning himself is never out of sight. But while this diminishes the genuinely dramatic character of the plays it does not necessarily diminish their interest. For exciting plots and life-like characters in whom their author's individuality is completely lost sight of, we Victorian readers look indeed far more to our prose novelists than to our verse playwrights ; and in poetry, when it is Mr. Browning who muses or analyses or indirectly holds up ideals or pronounces judgments—and at his clearest—some of us are disposed to say that we cannot easily have too much of him.

The idea of *Pippa Passes* is singularly fresh and simple. The fascinating little maiden who springs out of her attic-bed in the sunrise hour of New Year's Day, her one whole holiday in the year, has a day of achievements before her such as could rarely indeed fall to the lot of a little silk-winder ; and yet there is nothing in the least overstrained about it, and Pippa does not know a bit what she has done, and most likely never will know to the end of her life that she that day turned the course of four different sets of (to her) important people's lives.

Not a single golden moment of the day must be lost, but how spend it best? thinks Pippa, dressing. She, poor, solitary, bright-hearted child, will for once fancy herself possessed of the love that enfolds the ' happiest four ' in Asolo. First there is Ottima, whose wealthy husband owns the silk-mills, and whose lover, Sebald, is at her command. But there is scandal in this love—

> ' there's better love, I know !
> This foolish love was only day's first offer.'

The next she chooses shall be Phene's, the bride whose young sculptor-husband weds her that day. Yet even a husband's love may grow cold—only a parent's lasts on without change.

> 'Let me be cared about, kept out of harm,
> And schemed for, safe in love as with a charm.

She, fatherless and motherless from her infancy, will this evening be Luigi, watched by his mother's tender love. Best of all, and most lasting, is God's love, such as will bless the holy Bishop who is to rest to-night in his dead brother's palace.   To-night Pippa will be Monsignor.

Yet no ! for does she not already possess God's love shed on her own small self without need of fancy ?   What says the New Year's hymn ?

> 'All service ranks the same with God :
> . .. . God's puppets, best and worst,
> Are we ; there is no last nor first.'

So she will only pass by each, and see their happiness without envy—

> ' Being just as great, no doubt !
> Useful to men and dear to God as they ! '

Happy in her bright day, and mocking a little at herself, off she sets.

Away in the villa on the hillside Ottima and Sebald have this night murdered her aged husband, and now in the early morning they speak together of their crime.   Sebald is shaken and half remorseful.   Ottima, perfectly reckless, labours with feverish passion to revive his love for her ; she has all but hardened him, when above the sound of guilty vows rings Pippa's voice carolling her cheery little song as she loiters by and plucks a straggling heart's-ease from Ottima's clump—

> 'The year's at the spring,
> And day's at the morn :
>   *   *   *
> God's in His heaven—
> All's right with the world ! '

God's in his heaven ! The simple words light up for Sebald
what he is and what he has done as with a flash of heaven's
own light.

> ' I see what I have done,
> Entirely now ! Oh, I am proud to feel
> Such torments—let the world take credit thence—
> I, having done my deed, pay too its price ! '

Through his stinging conviction of sin, even Ottima's
conscience is aroused ; both are saved in spirit.

A little later, and Jules, the young sculptor, has led home
his beautiful bride only to find that he has been wickedly
duped by envious fellow-students and entrapped into marrying an ignorant girl of the lowest class. But before her
own lips have betrayed the secret, his first words have
awakened her torpid soul to see the goodness of the man
to whom this thing has been done, and to long for his
regenerating influence.

> ' What rises is myself,
> Not me the shame and suffering ; but they sink,
> Are left, I rise above them. Keep me so,
> Above the world ! '

None the less he is bidding her leave him, provided with
all the money he can raise to give her, when Pippa's voice
is heard, singing this time a little love-ballad. Somehow
the little song suggests to Jules a nobler part. Why not
keep to this woman who has such need of him ?

> ' Shall to produce form out of unshaped stuff
> Be art—and further, to evoke a soul
> From form be nothing? This new soul is mine ! '

The two depart to begin a new life and new pursuit of art
in ' some isle with the sea's silence on it.'

Later still, and Luigi, the ardent patriot, the inborn lover of nature who heeds the cuckoo's voice even while life and death depend upon his talk, debates with his mother the mission that in the council of conspirators has fallen to his lot. Shall he fulfil it and put the Austrian Emperor to death? Neither of them guess that Luigi will be arrested unless, by leaving home that night, he proves that the passport issued is really for his own use; and his mother anxiously, eagerly, dissuades him. She has almost prevailed by the mention of his betrothed, but Pippa turns the scale. She is singing again; and now it is a song of wisdom and justice in high places, of grace and peace reigning where with ' old smiling eyes '

'The king judged, sitting in the sun.'

The thought of his own country, down-trodden and oppressed under the foreign tyrant rushes back upon Luigi and stirs the old aspirations to free his land.

''Tis God's voice calls : how could I stay? Farewell !'

And now, late at night, the Bishop, so hallowed in Pippa's innocent imagination, sits in the palace of the dead brother whose wealth he inherits, closeted with an Intendant, the tool of that brother's crimes. Grasping for himself after riches that have been the price of this man's services, he threatens the Intendant with exposure and destruction for the murder of the infant child and heiress left by an elder brother years before. The Intendant turns upon him with news that the child still lives—''tis but a little black-eyed pretty singing Felippa, gay silk-winding girl '—Pippa herself—and then in return for undisturbed possession of his ill-gotten gains he offers to dispose of her after a new and fiendish plan of his own devising.

Her fate trembles in the balance, when once more the clear young voice rises from the street below in sweet words of simple love and knowledge of simple things—trees and grass and changing white moon. The Bishop's better side is touched; at his hasty order the villain is instantly bound and gagged, the very act commits the Bishop himself to a course of justice and restitution.

Back in her attic, Pippa thinks over the day she has spent, a little drearily perhaps, for the holiday is over, and naturally she is tired, and she has no suspicion of her real share in the day's events, or of any prospect in store for her other than twelve long months of monotonous silk-winding. She wonders how near she might ever approach these others—

> ' Approach, I mean, so as to touch them, so
> As to . . . in some way . . . move them—if you please,
> Do good or evil to them in some slight way.'

Perhaps silk of her winding may hem Ottima's cloak ! And how about the morning's dreams of importance ? But no doubt the hymn is right in some sense or other ; and she drops asleep with its words again upon her lips.

> ' *All service ranks the same with God—*
> *With God, whose puppets, best and worst,*
> *Are we : there is no last nor first.*'

It will be noticed how much the slightness in themselves of Pippa's songs does to carry out the main idea of the play—in Emerson's words.

> ' There is no great and no small
> To the soul that maketh all.'

Colombe's Birthday is again the story of a single day, in which a sudden sharp crisis puts more than one soul to the proof.   Colombe of Ravestein has been installed under her father's will as Duchess of Juliers and Cleves, but as the Duchy is held under Salic law, it is known—vaguely by herself, clearly by her courtiers—that her title cannot be maintained against the claim of her distant cousin, Prince Berthold, should he choose to assert it.   On the first anniversary of her investment, also her birthday, the letter containing his claim is received at the palace ; he himself will be there an hour or two later.   As the courtiers debate who shall present this unwelcome letter to the Duchess, a travel-stained advocate forces his way in, bearing a petition concerning grievances from Cleves, and entreats permission to lay it before the Duchess.   Leave is given on condition that he also presents the letter, which, in ignorance of its contents, he easily consents to do.   His outburst of indignant loyalty on discovering the part he has been made to play at once dismays the courtiers, wins the Lady Colombe to declare she will hold by her Duchy for the sake of remaining his sovereign, and constitutes him her counsellor.   Prince Berthold, greeted with this surprising intelligence, yet secure in his own right, courteously with-draws till Valence, the advocate, shall have had time to master the claims put forward in papers now left with him. Before their appointed meeting in the evening takes place, three things have happened.   Valence has discovered that the Prince's claims are indefeasible ; Prince Berthold has discovered that it would be more politic as well as pleasanter to win the Dukedom by marrying instead of dispossessing his spirited young cousin ; the courtiers think they have discovered that Colombe means to marry Valence, and know that by marriage with a subject her right would, by her father's will, pass to her kinsman.   Instead of demanding her Duchy, therefore, Berthold commissions Valence to offer Colombe his hand, which Valence, stifling his own feelings, does with conscientious eloquence. But on being pressed to say that Berthold *loves* the Duchess, he has to own that the offer is purely one of policy; and further admits that he sees the absence of love in Berthold through knowledge of his own love. For the moment Colombe loses all her delight in his devotion. She had thought it was disinterested loyalty, and behold, 'mere love'! She 'did ill to mistrust the world so soon'; she will hear Berthold speak for himself. The Prince, soon to be Emperor, repeats his splendid offer, not disguising that only splendour, not love, is his to give. At this point the courtiers, anxious to win the new sovereign's favour, break in with their fancied discovery of the state of feeling between Colombe and Valence, asking how service such as his could have been rendered except for love, or requited except by love. The Prince, unmoved, pits his magnificent rank and wealth against Valence's love, without a misgiving about the result. Valence, warned that his suit can but damage his lady's interests, is summoned to press or renounce it. The Duchess has had time to think since her first hasty vexation with his avowal of love; she has had the opportunity of comparing her two suitors; she has heard the courtiers' praise of Valence—true in fact, though false in motive—and now the unselfish tenderness and dignity with which he resigns her to Berthold lead to her instant decision, and Colombe declares—

> 'I take him—give up Juliers and the world.
> This is my Birthday.'

Such is the skeleton of the play. Its charm lies chiefly

in showing how at the touch of the mind of Valence, Colombe's is awakened into sudden and beautiful develop-ment.   In the past year Colombe, in spite of a little regretful longing for the river-side flowers and simple life of her old home, has been innocently happy in her new state, enjoying the deference of her little court, and entirely believing in its sincerity.   The wrongs and sufferings of Cleves, and the burning pity with which Valence makes them known, are alike a revelation to her; so, in another way, is the desertion of her courtiers so soon as it appears that her rule will be superseded.   With Valence at her side, she learns from these to distinguish between true and false grounds of rule—

> 'There is a vision in the heart of each
>   Of justice, mercy, wisdom, tenderness
>   To wrong and pain, and knowledge of its cure :
>   And these embodied in a woman's form
>   That best transmits them, pure as first received,
>   From God above her, to mankind below.
>   Will you derive your rule from such a ground,
>   Or rather hold it by the suffrage, say,
>   Of this man—this—and this ?'

Just when the hollowness of what she has hitherto supposed to be real loyalty, in showing itself has prepared her to yield up her Duchy willingly, a vision of what true dominion might be and do, decides her (although she perceives that outward government is not indispensable to its exercise) not to resign Juliers without testing the strength of her claim.   Already she avows—

> ' This is indeed my birthday—soul and body.
>   Its hours have done on me the work of years.'

But there is much more to come.   Valence has aroused in her a vivid perception of the blessings that a noble rule

can confer ; a marriage with Berthold might seem to offer
the largest possible scope for such a rule ; the question
now is, whether Colombe can rightly discriminate for herself
between the two lots open to her. And here we are
confronted with a new interest in the contrasting characters
of Berthold and Valence. Berthold is no ignoble man of
greed, no mere foil to Valence. On the contrary, the
description Valence gives of him is sometimes quoted as
being Browning's ideal of manhood.

> ' He gathers earth's whole good into his arms ;
>   Standing as man now, stately, strong and wise,
>   Marching to fortune, not surprised by her.
>   One great aim, like a guiding-star, above—
>   Which tasks strength, wisdom, stateliness, to lift
>   His manhood to the height that takes the prize ;
>   A prize not near—lest overlooking earth
>   He rashly spring to seize it—nor remote,
>   So that he rest upon his path content ;
>   But day by day while shimmering grows shine,
>   And the faint circlet prophesies the orb,
>   He sees so much as, just evolving these,
>   The stateliness, the wisdom and the strength,
>   To due completion, will suffice this life,
>   And lead him at his grandest to the grave.'

This sounds truly magnificent ; but on looking more
closely into even this passage, I think we shall see that to
regard it as Browning's ideal is to be misled by sound. The
word ' completion ' is in itself enough to arouse suspicion.
We have seen that with Browning completion in this life
means stagnation.[1] Again, ' he sees so much as will . . .

---

[1] Compare this effect of a too-perfect career with the effect of
Greek Art in *Old Pictures in Florence*. We have to remember that
the dramas are earlier work than the monologues, and that ideas in
them are often more fully worked out in the latter.

lead him at his grandest *to the grave.*' That is not usually the goal of Browning's thoughts. Often enough he looks forward to *death*, but it is as *re-birth*, another step onwards and upwards, for which the mouldering, all-terminating 'grave' is no synonym. There is even a flavour of scorn in the words. And this impression is fully confirmed as we read further in the same passage—

> ' So, mounting, feels each step he mounts,
>   Nor, as from each to each exultingly
>   He passes, overleaps one grade of joy.
>
> This for his own good :—with the world each gift
> Of God and man,—reality, tradition,
> Fancy and fact—so well environ him,
> That as a mystic panoply they serve—
> Of force, untenanted, to awe mankind,
> And work his purpose out with half the world,
> While he, their master, dexterously slipt
> From such encumbrance, is meantime employed
> With his own prowess in the other half.'

' *This for his own good*,'—a clear indication of what is wrong. And finally—

> ' Thus shall he go on, greatening, till he ends—
>   The man of men, the spirit of all flesh,
>   The fiery centre of an earthly world !'

No word of what is to come afterwards. ' He ends.' Berthold is indeed a sublimated type of worldly success at its loftiest; and Valence—true advocate—exhibits the loftiness in such a glamour of poetry that it is almost true to say he disguises the worldliness. Colombe is at first to some extent misled; but the weak point, the something wanting, which nullifies all the grandeur and glory of the rest, comes out later. He has no love, not even for Colombe. Valence admits—

> ' Had that been—love might so incline the Prince
> To the world's good, the world that's at his foot—
> I do not know, this moment, I should dare
> Desire that you refused the world—and Cleves—
> The sacrifice he asks.'

Through Melchior, Prince Berthold's book-loving, privileged friend, we learn more of the good in him. Melchior knows him thoroughly, counts him the ' one hero of the world '—

> —' one friend worth my books,
> Sole man I think it pays the pains to watch,'

and knowing the fine qualities that are going to waste in him, he leaves his books again and again to warn and persuade. As the two ride together into Juliers, Melchior laments Berthold's easy advance in worldly position by the help of his powerful relatives, and covets difficulties for him, and less material aims. Had he

> ' Conquered a footing inch by painful inch,—
> And, after long years' struggle, pounced at last
> On her for prize,—the right life had been lived,
> And justice done to divers faculties
> Shut in that brow.'

Again when Berthold has sent the offer of his hand to Colombe, Melchior tries to modify his cold-blooded desire for the marriage only because his cousin will make a suitable consort and be hindered by it from carrying claims against him from court to court, which her beauty might render dangerous to his future success. And once more at the close Melchior seems to appeal to the Prince's generosity to leave Colombe her Duchy when she weds her love—

> ' Speak, for I know you through your Popes and Kings ! '

But he does not succeed with Berthold as Valence with Colombe, partly perhaps because he was scarcely the same living proof of his own words, partly because the conditions were harder.   For Berthold has, as he thinks, already had his eyes opened when in the days of his obscurity the girl he wooed 'under the grey convent-wall' forsook him for a Brabant lord.

> 'I am past illusion on that score.'

He now views other minds through the distorting medium of this too hastily-accepted conviction, and utterly misreads them.   He mistakes Valence's consternation on hearing his offer for amazement at the honour it confers upon Colombe; in spite of Melchior he frankly rests his merits with Colombe on the worldly advantages he can give her—

> 'You will be Empress, once for all : with me
> The Pope disputes supremacy—you stand,
> And none gainsays, the earth's first woman.'

He is secure that 'the Empire wins' just before Colombe announces her decision; and when at last his error is laid bare, it is too late to save him—he is too fully committed to his worldly walks.

> 'I could not imitate—I hardly envy—
> I do admire you.'

He cannot even respond to Melchior's appeal; he can only remind Colombe with some humiliation that he needs her Duchy more than she does, and then prepare to plod on in the old way, though

> 'A somewhat wearier life seems to remain
> Than I thought possible.'

Valence on the other hand is destitute of everything that

Berthold has to give. He is poor, unknown, 'a nameless
advocate,' unfriended except by unhappy, starving Cleves;
and at first the discovery of his love for her has only
repelled Colombe. But his devotion to Cleves has given
her a new conception of possibilities in life, and has
suddenly quickened her power of judging between his
aspirations and the gilded but miserable aims that end in
self. The sincerity of his self-forgetting loyalty both to
Cleves and to Colombe is tried to the uttermost; he is
spared no test, however severe. He despises toil and
contention for the sake of Cleves; he stands fast by
Colombe when her false friends desert her; he is assailed
by temptation to pronounce her no Duchess, that station
may not divide them—and flings it away; next, knowing
beyond doubt that

> 'She has no shade of right
> To the distinction which divided us,'

he begins to hope that without treachery to Cleves she may
yet be his, and instantly his dawning hope is dashed by
Berthold's offer, which he himself must place in its most
attractive light before Colombe,—and he does it. A little
later, and ambiguous words persuade him that Colombe has
left him, him, flung his heart aside, 'the ermine o'er a
heartless breast embraced.' He is shaken with grief for

> 'this farewell to Heaven,
> Welcome to earth—this taking death for life—
> This spurning love and kneeling to the world'—

but even then not only refuses to press his own love against
her mistaken choice—'for what am I but hers, to choose
as she?'—but is too absolutely loyal to allow her image to
be dimmed or dethroned in his mind.

'Is the knowledge of her nought? the memory, nought?
—Lady, should such an one have looked on you,
Ne'er wrong yourself so much as quote the world
And say, love can go unrequited here !
You will have blessed him to his whole life's end—
Low passions hindered, baser cares kept back,
All goodness cherished where you dwelt—and dwell.

     *   *   *   ·   *

He wishes you no need, thought, care of him—
Your good, by any means, himself unseen,
Away, forgotten ! '

What depth of hidden anguish this last word covers ! Self-effacement could go no farther in Colombe's cause ; but yet one test remains for Cleves. Berthold, secure of victory, promises Valence whatever he shall ask. He might possess the flowers Colombe wears, or ask—

'One last touch of her hand I never more
    Shall see ;'

but the momentary struggle ends in his request—

'Cleves' Prince, redress the wrongs of Cleves ! '

Valence himself has risen through his love ; he is as faithful as before to Cleves, and at far heavier cost.

Such are the two men Colombe has to read, and we know the end. Valence has awakened her perception, 'evolved' her love ; she sees now unerringly, decides on the instant.

The principal ordeal has its echo amongst the courtiers. Guibert's wavering loyalty is first strengthened by the fine conduct of Valence ; then base motives are suggested which he believes too easily, and is disillusioned ; but the final issue more than restores him, he springs forward to follow Colombe into her self-chosen obscurity, levelling a parting shaft at his rival.

'God save you, Gauçelme ! 'Tis my Birthday, too ! '

One is sinfully glad that the remaining courtiers are likely to have no easy time under their new master, or rather his deputy, 'the black Barnabite!'

The pathetic tragedy of *The Blot in the 'Scutcheon* is no less direct and intelligible than these two beautiful little plays; and indeed none of the plays are really difficult. But we must turn now to Mr. Browning's longest work, *The Ring and the Book*.

The story of it can be told quite shortly. Crossing a Square in Florence one day Mr. Browning singled out on a stall of miscellaneous wares, a shabby little volume containing, partly in print and partly in manuscript, the full account of a murder case tried in Rome in February 1698. The accused was a nobleman of Arezzo, Count Guido Franceschini, who on the night of Christmas Eve, with four cut-throats in his pay, entered a lonely villa on the outskirts of Rome, stabbed his wife, a girl of seventeen, just a fortnight after the birth of their son, left her for dead, and murdered also the old couple who had brought her up, calling themselves her parents. In justification of the crime (the murderers having been taken red-handed before they could cross the boundaries), outraged honour was pleaded, it being alleged that the Count's wife, Pompilia, had left his house eight months earlier in company with a handsome young priest who had brought her to Rome. But Pompilia survived her wounds for four days, and from her own account and the evidence of others it appeared that the Count had been guilty of diabolical cruelty towards her, and had finally, by dint of forged letters, set a trap for her, intending to drive her into a position that would enable him to get rid of her by a divorce, still keeping her fortune, which divorce he had tried and failed to obtain. It was urged further that Pompilia and the Canon had never spoken to each other until the time when her appeal for help moved him to aid her escape to her parents' house in Rome, and that both were blameless. The Court decreed death, to Count Guido and his accomplices; but as he, though a layman, had taken some steps towards priest's orders, an appeal in his favour was carried to the Pope, Innocent XII. The Pope having reviewed the whole case, with the evidence and pleadings on both sides, gave orders that the Count and his four hired assassins should at once be executed in the most public spot in Rome.

This, in bare outline, is the tragic story which, as he read on and on in the little old book, took living hold of Browning's imagination—'deep calling unto deep.' Every scene acted itself over again in his mind that day; and he spent the next four years in so shaping the facts of the 'old woe' caught up and saved from rubbish-heaps of the past, that it should live anew in men's minds, even penetrate the minds of the 'British Public—ye who like me not.' At the end of the four years he presented that public with his poem of *The Ring and the Book*, the symbolic title signifying that as the artificer in gold mixes alloy with the pure metal too soft by itself to bear file and hammer, but when the ring is fashioned drives off the alloy with acid, leaving pure gold again; so, conversely, the poet has tempered the hard crude facts of the Florentine book with his own interpreting imagination, and having thus welded, wrought, and stamped them, fancy, which was needed only to help in workmanship, not to eke out substance, disappears, leaving a rounded whole of unmixed truth. At this point Mr. Browning exclaims—

'A ring without a posy, and that ring mine?'

and then breaks into an apostrophe to his dead wife in which the sober blank verse metre becomes instinct with lyrical passion. The first two lines especially are like nothing else in all his poetry.

> ' O lyric Love, half angel and half bird
> And all a wonder and a wild desire,—
> Boldest of hearts that ever braved the sun,
> Took sanctuary within the holier blue,
> And sang a kindred soul out to his face,—
> Yet human at the red-ripe of the heart—
> When the first summons from the darkling earth
> Reached thee amid thy chambers, blanched their blue,
> And bared them of the glory—to drop down,
> To toil for man, to suffer or to die,—
> This is the same voice : can thy soul know change ?
> Hail then, and hearken from the realms of help !
> Never may I commence my song, my due
> To God who best taught song by gift of thee,
> Except with bent head and beseeching hand—
> That still, despite the distance and the dark,
> What was, again may be ; some interchange
> Of grace, some splendour once thy very thought,
> Some benediction anciently thy smile :
> —Never conclude, but raising hand and head
> Thither where eyes, that cannot reach, yet yearn
> For all hope, all sustainment, all reward,
> Their utmost up and on,—so blessing back
> In those thy realms of help, that heaven thy home,
> Some whiteness which, I judge, thy face makes proud,
> Some wanness where, I think, thy foot may fall ! '

The story of the trial and the events that led up to it, with full accessories of episodes and details, is told from ten different points of view. It is hard to imagine how the strange medley of qualities, bad and good, the tangle of base and noble motives in human affairs which it was Browning's unfailing delight to study, could have been more effectually focussed. Greed, craft, hate, vacillation, cynicism, ripe wisdom, indomitable purity, and a hundred others play their part in a tragedy that appeals to the deepest springs of human conduct and feeling. Incidentally too, Browning's intimate knowledge of Italian life and history has free scope, and we get vivid glimpses into the ways of Roman and provincial society in the seventeenth century. There is the needy nobleman wasting years in vain attendance upon the chances of a Church sinecure, far enough advanced towards Orders to be eligible for a profitable office, yet not too deeply committed to be able to resort to a marriage for wealth ; there are careless governors, unfaithful priests ; there is the worldly, frivolous Canon, petted by fashion, yet noble at heart and capable of better things ; the conscientious Augustine friar ; the nuns, not beyond temptation to lose sight of truth and charity at a prospect of gain to their convent ; there are the nimble-witted lawyers, pleading their case with Latin and eloquence and technical *finesse ;* the eminent personages to be met in Roman drawing-rooms ; the paid assassins so easily found ; the populace of Rome.

We have first the view of the pending trial taken by ' Half-Rome,' whose spokesman lounges away with his fellows from the Corso where the murdered peasants' bodies are laid, to gossip at ease over the event. They find much excuse for Count Guido as a victim of imposture, for did not the old woman Violante pass off upon Pietro her husband as her own daughter a girl picked up from the streets ? and did not the couple after marrying her to Guido as an heiress, seek to defraud him by declaring Pompilia's true origin ? and did not the girl herself confirm the character of her real parentage and well-founded suspicions of her own

conduct when she quitted her ill-used husband in company
with the very Canon who had roused his jealousy? and
had not the law itself failed him when in punishment it
merely secluded the wife in the care at first of a sisterhood
of nuns, and then of her nominal parents, and exiled the
Canon for a while to Civita? And if further evidence were
needed, the Count had it on that Christmas night when at
the sound of Canon Caponsacchi's name the door flew
hospitably open to receive him. How is it possible to
blame the husband who, in such a case, takes the law into
his own hands? He must be acquitted; and one of
Browning's inimitable humorous touches, which explain so
much in a word, closes this discourse when the speaker
commends the vindicated revenge to the notice of a certain
neighbour over-attentive in serenading the house where 'I
keep a wife,' adding parenthetically to a bystander,

('You, being his cousin, may go tell him so.')

'The Other Half-Rome' speaks next, and instinctively
takes Pompilia's side. No doubt Violante's deception was
wrong, yet her desire to secure Pompilia's prosperous future
was surely excusable; and for Pompilia herself, poor child,
married at thirteen (through the wily schemes of Guido
and his brothers practised on her guardians) to the grim
Count from whose violence she is driven to appeal for
protection to the governor of Arezzo, to the Archbishop, to
Guido's brother Abate Paolo, to a priest in confession—and
all in vain—what but pity can be felt for her? The letters
alleged to have passed between her and Caponsacchi are
clearly forgeries, since Pompilia can neither read nor write,
and as clearly prove her husband's intrigues. Then observe
how his courage failed at the very moment when, if really

wronged, it should have risen highest ; at the moment when
he overtook his wife and the Canon at the Castelnuovo
wayside inn on their flight to Rome, and instead of taking
instant vengeance, was cowed by them, and resorted to an
appeal to law where misleading evidence might weigh.
And then how craftily he delayed his final vengeance until
all rights in the disputed marriage-portion were his through
the infant son whose birth turned intervening lives into
mere obstructions to be disposed of with all possible speed !
Guido is the common enemy ; if law be worth anything, he
must die.

So reason the common folk ; neither side having anything
sounder to go upon than prepossessions that bias their
judgment in one direction or the other. Next we have
the more critical, balanced judgment representing Roman
education and refinement. 'Tertium Quid' speaks to an
Excellency and a Highness, and is guarded in his utterances.
On the whole

> 'Quality took the decent side, of course ;

would, in the interests of domestic propriety and discipline,
defend the husband's rights and excuse his faults, partly
natural to a man of his rank. Still no doubt he had gone
to an extreme in his conduct, though not without serious
provocation. There have been faults on both sides; and
Tertium Quid, dispassionate and neutral, declines to
pronounce decisively for either.

Then comes the trial itself. Count Guido, fresh from
torture under which he has admitted his crime, speaks first
in his own defence; he is followed by Caponsacchi,
summoned from Civita to repeat the account he had given
of his relations with Pompilia at the early enquiry which

had taken place at Guido's instance immediately after their flight from Arezzo. To this succeeds Pompilia's own story of her life, whispered with painful breathings from the bed where she lay dying. Next we have the written defence of Guido put in by his counsel, Dominus Hyacinthus de Archangelis, Procurator of the Poor, which, the murder being admitted, is directed to win a reprieve by extenuating his conduct in all particulars, from the legal point of view. Except as a doubtful case in law this advocate has evidently no interest in it whatever; he is a good-natured, unimpressionable man, much preoccupied with the thought of his eight-year old boy, whose birthday they are just going to celebrate at home with a supper of fried liver and parsley. Pompilia's official defender, Doctor Johannes Baptista Bottinius, the Fisc, or public prosecutor, is less careful to establish her fair fame, than to put the best colour on behaviour into which she might under the circumstances have been driven, and to prove Guido's guilt. He too is almost ostentatiously indifferent to all but the legal aspect of the case. The pleadings of the two lawyers, interlarded as they are with Latin quotations, ill-timed jokes, flippant personalities, are indeed the least interesting part of the work; but no doubt their display of keen though shallow cleverness, and their indifference to the heights and depths of the tragedy on whose fringes their wit is employed, do heighten the effect of the rest by force of contrast—though the contrast sometimes jars more than the humour relieves the strain of tragedy.

Judgment having gone against the Count, and an appeal having been carried to the Pope, we have next his review of the case, given after a minutely careful examination of all the pleadings. And when this has ended in an order for immediate execution of the five criminals, Guido throws off all disguise and pours out his cynical 'confession.' The history ends with certain letters describing the execution ; a plea from the Fisc that as the Court, though condemning Guido, had not pronounced Pompilia innocent, her inheritance passed by law to the Convent which had sheltered her, and a further instrument, due to the Pope, by which Pompilia's innocence was finally declared, and her inheritance secured to her son.

Among the crowd of persons and masses of detail collected in this great work, four characters stand conspicuously out,—Count Guido, Canon Caponsacchi, Pompilia, and the Pope.

To most of his contemporaries the circumstances, but imperfectly known, serve rather to disguise than demonstrate Guido's character ; but we, admitted to fuller knowledge, see that he is from first to last an appalling impersonation of cold-blooded, calculating cruelty and greed. Whatever small share of grace he might ever have possessed has all disappeared in the course of his thirty years 'of idle and envious waiting upon the chances of fortune ;. he is soured through and through by his fruitless efforts to appropriate the Church's loaves and fishes; his marriage is a money-hunting venture hit upon by his like-minded though feebler brothers. Afterwards his inventive cruelty wreaked upon his wife—

> ' putting, day by day, hour by hour,
> The untried torture to the untouched place,'

his intrigues against her, planned with Satanic craft and malice, are such as to call out the wise old Pope's exclamation of marvel at their failure—

> ' O God,
> Who shall pluck sheep Thou holdest, from Thy hand ? '

The wanton torture inflicted at last by his fiendish Genoese dagger, triangular in the blade,

> ' Armed with those little hook-teeth in the edge
> To open in the flesh nor shut again,'

is a true index to his conduct throughout—not only are his ends bad, but he takes the worst means to reach them. His ingenuity equals his ferocity. His defence before the Court is a masterpiece of special pleading and subtlety. He knows and plays upon the worst side of his judges under cover of a mock-humility; he skilfully confuses the issues; draws off attention from his own guilt to fix it upon any scrap of evidence that can be turned against his victims; simulates an agony of wounded honour and baffled fatherhood compared with which he declares the physical torture he has undergone to have been a positive relief; leads his hearer through mazes of sophistry where truth and falsehood lose all meaning, and right and wrong change places. But after the Pope's decision the real Guido shows himself. He flings away the mask, and pours out a recital of naked wickedness into the horror-stricken ears of Cardinal and Abate, while one strives to check him with the crucifix, and the other shudders over his beads to exorcise the powers of hell let loose, as it seems, in that desperate prisoner's cell. Among those who really know Guido, it takes Pompilia to find, I do not say one redeeming trait—not even Pompilia could find that—but one link with humanity, one point where human feeling other than detestation could go out to him. Incapable of malice herself, the worst she will say of the ' woeful man ' who has dragged her young life through an Inferno upon earth, and cut short the bright joy of her motherhood by a cruel death, is simply

> ' So he was made ; he nowise made himself :
> I could not love him, but his mother did.'

In forcible contrast to the Count's shifty defence comes
Canon Caponsacchi's burst of hot indignation. Why did
the Judges, now so anxious for his witness, not believe the
story as he told it eight months before? What had come of
their contempt for his warning of the danger that threatened
Pompilia?—of their careless, vaunted guardianship?

> 'I left Pompilia to your watch and ward,
> And now you point me—there and thus she lies!'

Why had he ever allowed himself to leave her in their
hands?—or, most bitter of all, suffered Guido to escape
when within arm's-reach? And then he once more
describes the frivolous, dissipated life from which in one
supreme moment a single glance of Pompilia's had awakened
him to a shame-stricken sense of his desecrated priesthood,
and bowed him down in reverent worship of her saintliness.
He tells of the love-letters, forged, as he instantly detected
of the one genuine summons, when he found her standing
lamp in hand above him like Our Lady of all the Sorrows;
of the appeal to his protection which had pierced him with
pity and roused every instinct of his manliness to rescue
her; of their flight, and the words stamped into his soul
as they fell, which now and again had broken the silent
tension; of the pause at Castelnuovo when Pompilia,
awakened out of the dead sleep of exhaustion to find her
defender in the threatening clutches of her husband, had
sprung to seize and wield Guido's sword herself, and when
overpowered and disarmed, had uttered a sublime defiance
before which the tyrant slunk away abashed.[1] The rest

---

[1] This scene irresistibly recalls the climax of *Instans Tyrannus*—

> 'Do you see? Just my vengeance complete,
>   The man sprang to his feet,
> Stood erect, caught at God's skirts, and prayed!
>   —So, *I* was afraid!'

they know only too well.   Again and again Caponsacchi's
anguish breaks out, and is repressed lest it should injure
Pompilia with the coarse-minded Judges—for himself he
cares nothing any more for their awards.

> 'I have done with being judged.
> I stand here guiltless in thought, word and deed,
> To the point that I apprise you,—in contempt
> For all misapprehending ignorance.
> O' the human heart, much more the mind of Christ,—
> That I assuredly did bow, was blessed
> By the revelation of Pompilia.   There!
> Such is the final fact I fling you, Sirs.'

But when all is finished his imagination wanders off to a
dream of what life *might* have been to him unfettered by
the vow of his calling, companioned by *her*.

> 'To have to do with nothing but the true,
> The good, the eternal—and these, not alone
> In the main current of the general life,
> But small experiences of every day,
> Concerns of the particular hearth and home :
> To learn not only by a comet's rush,
> But a rose's birth,—not by the grandeur, God—
> But the comfort, Christ.'

He would fain pass calmly from the happy dream to his
grey destiny of solitude, but suddenly all his strength breaks
down in one heart-broken cry—

> 'O great, just, good God !   Miserable me !'

In the character of Pompilia, some hold that Mr.
Browning's creative genius touches flood-mark. He has
drawn many another as life-like and consistent, but none
quite so difficult, none so flawlessly beautiful, none that
would have been so marred by a single false phrase.   For
her childlike simplicity is never lost in the depth of her

power to endure, discern, and when need be, to dare. The happy, innocent child of thirteen is passed through a four years' ordeal of steadily intensifying misery, due to no fault of her own, culminating in almost hourly peril to body and soul, and the supreme test of sudden and painful death at the very moment when life has at last become precious to her, finds her stainless, unembittered, full of love and holy trust. The pitiful side of Rome sees the pathetic element as she lies with rent body in 'the good house that helps the poor to die'—

> 'Little Pompilia with the patient brow
> And lamentable smile on those poor lips'—

but there is much more to see. Her husband, loathing the whiteness he cannot smirch, and the endurance he cannot ruffle, speaks of her as 'the pale poison my hasty hunger took for food.'

> 'What you call my wife
> I call a nullity in female shape.'

He compares her to a picture by Fra Angelico,

> 'Who traces you some timid chalky ghost
> That turns the church into a charnel.'

But in spite of himself he is compelled to dread the meaning of her patience—

> 'I advise—no one think to bear that look
> Of steady wrong endured as steadily
> Through what sustainment of deluding hope?
> Who is the friend i' the background that notes all?
> Who may come presently to close accounts?
> This self-possession to the uttermost,
> How does it differ in aught, save degree,
> From the terrible patience of God?'

And his secret recognition of her true nature, unacknowledged even to himself before, is forced out in his last wild appeal when he is claimed by the stern Brotherhood of Death—

> ' Abate,—Cardinal,—Christ,—Maria,—God, . . .
> Pompilia, will you let them murder me ? '

Pompilia, dead, stands highest in his thoughts of Godlike power and divine compassion.

Of the passion of worship she inspires in Canon Caponsacchi we have already seen a little ; but even he cannot estimate her so fully as the clear-sighted, sage old Pope, who knows her whole story. And as he blames Guido the more for having sinned against the light of his birth, training, associations, so he finds Pompilia's purity and patience and faith and forgiving temper the more remarkable because of her unfavourable entrance into life. He understands the rare virtue of one who, resisting nothing for her own sake, could change submission for heroic daring the moment another life than her own was imperilled ; and where all is praised, he praises most in her that having been ' dutiful to the foolish parents first, submissive next to the bad husband,' tolerant even of the miserable tools who wreaked his will upon her, she could yet rise from the old law to new service—

> ' Not
> To longer bear, but henceforth fight, be found
> Sublime in new impatience with the foe !
> Endure man and obey God : plant firm foot
> On neck of man, tread man into the hell
> Meet for him, and obey God all the more ! '

His wonder grows as he observes how this 'woman-child' has combined with her child's intellect the unerring spiritual insight of a veteran saint.

Oh child that didst despisè thy life so much
When it seemed only thine to keep or lose,
How the fine ear felt fall the first low word,
" Value life, and preserve life for My sake ! "

  * * * * *

     ' Didst hear, comprehend,
Accept the obligation laid on thee,
Mother elect, to save the unborn child.

  * * * * *

      ' Didst resist—
Anticipate the office that is mine—
And with his own sword stay the upraised arm,
The endeavour of the wicked, and defend
Him who,—again in my default,—was there
For visible providence : one less true than thou
To touch, i' the past, less practised in the right,
Approved less far in all docility
To all instruction,—how had such an one
Made scruple " Is this motion a decree ? "
It was authentic to the experienced ear
O' the good and faithful servant.'

Pompilia's religious love for her child, told in her own
straightforward, simple way, breathes the holy warmth and
calm trustfulness of a Madonna.

' I never realized God's birth before—
How He grew likest God in being born.
This time I felt like Mary, had my babe
Lying a little on my breast like hers.

  * * * * *

     ' We poor
Weak souls, how we endeavour to be strong !
I was already using up my life,—
This portion, now, should do him such a good,
This other go to keep off such an ill !
The great life ; see, a breath and it is gone !
So is detached, so left all by itself
The little life, the fact which means so much.
Shall not God stoop the kindlier to His work,

His marvel of creation, foot would crush,
Now that the hand He trusted to receive
And hold it, lets the treasure fall perforce?
The better; He shall have in orphanage
His own way clearlier; if my babe
Outlived the hour—and he has lived two weeks—
It is through God who knows I am not by.
Who is it makes the soft gold hair turn black,
And sets the tongue, might lie so long at rest,
Trying to talk?   Let us leave God alone!
Why should I doubt He will explain in time
What I feel now, but fail to find the words?
My babe nor was, nor is, nor yet shall be
Count Guido Franceschini's child at all—
Only his mother's, born of love not hate!
So shall I have my rights in after-time.
It seems absurd, impossible to-day;
So seems so much else not explained but known!'

In the last few lines there is evidence of the assurance born
of insight too unclouded to be called faith, which has
governed her at all times; it is still plainer in her farewell
thoughts of Guido.

> ' *We shall not meet in this world nor the next,*
> But where will God be absent? In His face
> Is light, but in His shadow healing too:
> Let Guido touch the shadow and be healed!'

And lastly, Browning's doctrine of ideal love is made perfect
and revealed in Pompilia. As the shadow of death falls
upon her, she turns away from all else to spend her last
failing· breath in 'being true' to the man for whose truth
she has fought, whose rescuing hand saved her to save her
child, gave her months of healing peace, and her long,
whole fortnight of mother's bliss;—'my one friend, my
only, all my own.' For these two there could be no union
on earth, not a word of love even between them; but no

fault of theirs has either raised the separating barriers or
broken through them.   Their great love, deep, passionate,
unearthly, pure, is its own safeguard on earth, its own
warrant of fulfilment in the heavens.   And so without a sign
of struggle or of parting, Pompilia's word can teach him to
'wait God's instant men call years' in faithful tranquillity.

> 'O lover of my life, O soldier-saint,
>   No work begun shall ever pause for death!
>   Love will be helpful to me more and more
>   I' the coming course, the new path I must tread—
>   My weak hand in thy strong hand, strong for that!
>   *   *   *   *   *   *
>   Marriage on earth seems such a counterfeit,
>   Mere imitation of the inimitable :
>   In heaven we have the real and true and sure.'

They will be as the angels, 'who, apart, know themselves
into one.'   With this celestial love in her heart Pompilia's
closing words have the still rapture of one who at the
supreme moment beholds the unseen and is satisfied with it.

> 'Through such souls alone
> God stooping shows sufficient of His light
> For us i' the dark to rise by.   And I rise.'

Here at least, in modern English poetry is one woman
worthy to enter the bright brave ranks of Cordelia and
Desdemona, Isabella and Hermione and Juliet and Imogen ;
worthy to clasp their outstretched hands of welcome to a
soul well-tempered like their own.

Hardly less impressive, in a very different way, is the
venerable Pope, as, sitting in his austerely plain private
room, he deliberates alone at the close of the dreary winter's
day whose leaden hours have been devoted to judicial sifting
of the documentary evidence.   His mind is fully made up

now on the merits of the case; but one by one he mentally
summons up every actor in it, passing his judgment on
each; and then with searching care he tests the grounds of
his own confidence in the tremendously responsible decision
his office demands of him. His awards of blame and praise
are given with the mellowed wisdom of ripe experience;
they are carefully weighed, yet unhesitatingly clear and
decided. Of Guido's infamy and Pompilia's virtue he has
no shadow of doubt; but he looks rather anxiously at
Caponsacchi, gladdened by his prompt and noble response
to Pompilia's appeal, yet not blinded to its over-impulsive
character, which through undue and needless disregard of
decorum has laid them both open to evil misconstruction.
Many a fresh light does the Pope throw on what has passed,
as when he speaks of the letters

> 'false beyond all forgery—
> Not just handwriting and mere authorship,
> But false to body and soul they figure forth.'

And again when he unsparingly lays bare the moral guilt of
Guido's paid accomplices in the murder. But we must pass
on to notice, though but meagrely, one or two of the reflections that arise in him when, courageous as he is, a momentary hesitation to put in force his own decision drives him
to reconsider the grounds of his authority. With fresh
vigour he expounds the doctrine of life we have already
traced; his own misgiving puts him to the test—

> 'I am near the end; but still not at the end;
> All to the very end is trial in life:
> At this stage is the trial of my soul
> Danger to face, or danger to refuse?
> Shall I dare try the doubt now, or not dare?'

And again—

> 'Life is probation and the earth no goal
> But starting-point of man : compel him strive,
> Which means in man as good as reach the goal.'

Later on he connects the element of uncertainty (in Browning's view, as we have seen, a beneficent element) with the
hold that a divine creed takes of the hearts of men—

> 'What but the weakness in a faith supplies
> The incentive to humanity, no strength
> Absolute, irresistible, comports?
> How can man love but what he yearns to help?'

and thus gives a singular and unexpected application
to the apostolic saying, 'God hath chosen the weak things
of the world to confound the things which are mighty.'
With equal courage and originality, and very consistently,
after a sad review of the spiritual death around him which
the Church's outward success seems to have brought in its
wake, he goes on to forecast a possible renewal of life
through a new invasion of doubt.

> 'What if it be the mission of that age
> My death will usher into life, to shake
> This torpor of assurance from our creed,
> Re-introduce the doubt discarded, bring
> That formidable danger back, we drove
> Long ago to the distance and the dark?
> No wild beast now prowls round the infant camp ;
> We have built wall and sleep in city safe :
> But if some earthquake try the towers that laugh
> To think they once saw lions rule outside,
> And man stand out again, pale, resolute,
> Prepared to die,—which means alive at last?'

His own ordeal is past ; his doubt has been honestly
faced and overcome ; his decision is surer than ever.

> ' I smite
> With my whole strength once more, ere end my part,
> Ending, so far as man may, this offence.'

Then he gives a passing notice to the importunate and
plausible worldly reasons with which all fashionable Rome,
supported by the Emperor's Envoy, demand his pardon for
Guido. He does not stay or stoop to refute them; their
sufficient answer is contained in his order, despatched now
without another moment's delay, for the execution of the
five criminals.

He reflects gravely that his decree of immediate death
grants the one chance of salvation left to Guido—may give
him in its suddenness an instant's shock of blinding light,
the sole alternative to relegation

> 'Into that sad obscure sequestered state
> Where God unmakes but to remake the soul
> He else made first in vain.'

For the rest, his own duty is plain—

> ' Enough, for I may die this very night,
> And how should I dare die, this man let live?'

The poem carries many a lesson with it; and in a brief
epilogue Browning answers a question of high interest as
addressed to one who, among the poets, works so definitely
as a teacher.

> ' Why take the artistic way to prove so much?'

' Because,' he replies—

> 'Because, it is the glory and good of Art
> That Art remains the one way possible
> Of speaking truth, to mouths like mine at least.'

*　　*　　*　　*　　*

> 'Art may tell a truth
> Obliquely, do the thing shall breed the thought,
> Nor wrong the thought, missing the mediate word.
> So you may paint your picture . . .
>
> *   *   *   *   *
>
> So write a book shall mean beyond the facts,
> Suffice the eye and save the soul beside.'

So, with another word of dedication to his 'Lyric Love,'
ends this great work.

> 'It lives,
> If precious be the soul of man to man.'

Thorough-going students of Browning who have a fair
amount of spare time will not stop here.   They will dig for
more treasure in his earlier poems, *Sordello* and *Paracelsus*,
and in his later work, especially, it may be, in *Balaustion*
and the *Dramatic Idylls ;* but these are more difficult,
and it is perhaps better to assume that the busy people
for whom University Extension Lectures are in the main
intended, will spend what remains of their scanty leisure
more profitably on the master-works of other poets.   So far
as their *teaching* is concerned, there is the less reason to de-
plore an incomplete acquaintance with Browning's voluminous writings because his attitude as a thinker has remained
singularly unchanged.   The central lesson he presents so
variously remains the same throughout, a lesson of hope,
courage, strenuous aspiration.   Rightly he calls himself
in the final poem of his last volume of verse—

> 'One who never turned his back, but marched breast forward,
>   Never doubted clouds would break,
> Never dreamed, though right were worsted, wrong would triumph,
> Held we fall to rise, are baffled to fight better,
>   Sleep to wake.'

III.

ELIZABETH BARRETT BROWNING.

*' I was born to poet-uses,
To love all things set above me, all of good and all of fair.'*
Lady Geraldine's Courtship.

MRS. BROWNING'S poetry is so closely bound up with her
life that it is almost impossible to separate the two. She
was born in or about 1809 (there has been some controversy
about the exact year), a delicate, intelligent child, whose
chief delight as she grew into girlhood lay in eager study of
great books. Her own literary efforts began early, and were
helped by her father's encouragement ; but after the publication in 1826 of her first poems, of which the longest was an
Essay on Mind after the manner of Pope, there was a long
pause of seven years before the appearance of another
volume, this time a translation of *Prometheus Bound,* with
some miscellaneous original poems. In 1837 her health,
always feeble, was further weakened by the breakage of a
blood-vessel in the lungs ; and two years later the shock of
her eldest brother's death by drowning at Torquay, turned
her for years into a complete invalid. Confined to a sofa in
a darkened room to which only her closest friends were
admitted, she spent nearly seven years of cloister-like
seclusion in the one pursuit from which nothing could deter
her—insatiable reading and the cultivation of her own

poetical gifts. In 1842 came her marriage with Robert
Browning, to the consternation of her father, who was
never reconciled to it, notwithstanding the amazing im-
provement in her health which immediately falsified all
alarmist predictions. Her own intense happiness, helped
no doubt by the change of climate, seems to have given her
the rallying power she needed. She was at once carried off
to Italy, and there, first at Pisa, then in the famous home of
Casa Guidi, in Florence, were spent the fifteen years of a
marriage for which the whole world has been richer, not
only by the priceless treasure of a realised ideal, but for
the actual work accomplished in consequence of it. *His*
subsequent poems became, in his own words, a ' due '

' To God, who best taught song by gift of thee.'

To *her* it meant unlooked-for length of days, new development of powers. All Mrs. Browning's best work was inspired
by her marriage and the new life that followed.

Both in the way of success and of limitation, the manner
of her previous life has impressed clear signs upon her work.
It is most natural that one who lived in almost unbroken
retirement should have known too little of men and women
in the world for the requirements of drama, and therefore
not wonderful that *The Seraphim* and *A Drama of Exile*
should, in spite of fine passages, be failures dramatically.
Nor is it surprising that out-of-door nature should enter
comparatively little into poems whose author was to begin
with a fragile girl, and later, the constant inhabitant of a
sick-room. Her own words *To Flush* best record what that
meant—

' But of *thee* it shall be said,
This dog watched beside a bed

Day and night unweary,
Watched within a curtained room
Where no sunbeam brake the gloom
Round the sick and dreary.

*   *   *

' Other dogs in thymy dew
Tracked the hares and followed through
Sunny moor or meadow ;
This dog only, crept and crept
Next a languid cheek that slept,
Sharing in the shadow.'

The description is all the more touching because it is only as they affect her dog that it occurs to her to lament the privations of her lot.

On the other hand she was rarely too ill to read, and often well enough to write ; and having every possible alleviation that love could devise and wealth provide, her unquenchable craving for book-lore of every description had such opportunities of gratification as but few women have enjoyed. Even as a child, as she herself says, she ' ate and drank Greek,' and her enthusiasm for learning, old and new, grew with her growth, becoming only stronger as her bodily strength declined. Perhaps the power of her own mind is shown in nothing more plainly than in her mastery of such masses of reading without detriment to her creative gift. Her wide and sound learning told largely upon her work. Although as a rule those of her poems which show it most plainly in subject or allusions are not the most highly prized, yet one or two of her very best could never have been written without it ; and the immense indirect gain is clearly seen in her grasp, firm handling, powers of expression.

Here, however, we have to notice the effect upon Mrs. Browning's diction of knowledge drawn too exclusively from books. Its richness and beauty are seriously spoilt by the extraordinary words she frequently introduces. She hardly appears to know obsolete from words of present day use, and besides words such as 'unexpressive,' in the Miltonic sense, 'geste,' where no archaic effect is required, she brings in others far more questionable, such as 'reboant,' 'vatic,' 'aspectable'; and many which, like 'oftly,' 'processive,' 'conmoving,' 'inerned,' are of her own coinage. These peculiarities of diction belong chiefly to her early work; but even in the beautiful *Sonnets from the Portuguese* the music and the reader's attention are now and then disturbed by such a word as 'exanimate.' Other faults of style have been set down to over-hasty writing, or excused on the ground that only since her day has the standard of finish in English verse risen so high. But Mrs. Browning herself enters a deliberate and vigorous protest against having it supposed that she has written carelessly. 'If I fail,' she writes, 'it will not be because I have shrunk from the amount of labour—where labour could do anything. I have *worked* at poetry—it has not been with me reverie, but art.' Again she speaks of the revision her poems have undergone; and we have but to compare early and late editions to see how true this is. When her use of such rhymes as 'inherit—spirit,' 'month—loth,' 'tell us—Hellas,' 'islands—silence,' 'on—sun,' 'flowing—slow in,' was criticised, she answered by producing more of them; and defended them in a private letter as 'chosen, selected, on principle, and with the determinate purpose of doing my best. . . . A great deal of attention—far more than it would take to rhyme with conventional accuracy—have I given to the subject of rhymes.' After this, the rhymes may still be regarded as slipshod, but they cannot be called the result of slipshod haste in work. We are driven to feel that there must have been an inherently defective sense of style in a poet who, with the best models of Greek and Latin literature before her, writing at a time when her contemporary, Tennyson, was producing work of the most perfect finish that English poetry has ever reached, and possessing her own easy command of language, could deliberately choose halting rhymes ' on principle,' mar the music of ' the soul's expression,' by ill-fitting metres, misplaced pauses and accents, or spoil the unity of a poem, as the simplicity of *Bertha in the Lane* is spoilt, by two bombastic stanzas at the end.

Another effect of Miss Barrett's suffering life is shown in the sadness that pervades most of her poetry. Little wonder indeed.

> ' I have known how sickness bends,
>   I have known how sorrow breaks,—
> How quick hopes have sudden ends,
>   How the heart thinks till it aches
> Of the smile of buried friends.'

Every word of this kind is with her stamped with the truth and gravity of experience, as far as possible removed from any semi-morbid luxury of simulated grief. And in her case grief has come upon one able not only to bear with courage and sweetness, but to analyse and interpret, and so we get from her utterances at once quick with feeling and weighty with suggestive thought, as in that finest of her sonnets in which she questions the new love whether it will fill to her the place of all she leaves for it, even the place sacred to memories of the dead.

> ' That's hardest.   If to conquer love, has tried,
> To conquer grief, tries more, as all things prove ;
> For grief indeed is love and grief beside.'

It is indeed through her acquaintance and sympathy with

grief that Mrs. Browning works most powerfully; her strength lies neither in narrative nor drama, nor even in her learning itself, though the possession of it does her signal service, but in fine expression of emotion,—pity, tenderness, indignation, and especially love, in every deepest and highest sense.

Mrs. Browning's originality begins to assert itself with her ballads. In these the influence of other poets is still perceptible, the setting of *Isobel's Child*, for example, often recalls Coleridge's *Christabel*, though the motive is entirely different—but it is less so than in *A Drama of Exile*, which is put at a disadvantage by the comparison it suggests with *Paradise Lost*. They are simpler and more human in conception than the somewhat cloudy *Seraphim;* and the grace and freedom of their execution, the generally skilful employment of enough and not too much archaism in language, their freshness, and a certain weird effect due partly to the situations imagined and partly to the glamour of language thrown over them, speedily made them popular. *The Romaunt of Margret, Romaunt of the Page, Lay of the Brown Rosary,* have each their special merits; but *The Rhyme of the Duchess May* stands highest. The tale is of a fair lady carried off by her lover from a marriage appointed and hateful to her, of furious kinsmen in pursuit, of the castle's siege and capture, and of the desperate leap on horseback, from the topmost battlements, of its lord and the new-made wife who would not be parted from him. The description of leading the splendid war-horse up to the battlements, and his behaviour there, is especially fine.

> 'And a look of human woe from his staring eyes did go,
> *Toll slowly.*
> And a sharp cry uttered he, in a foretold agony
> Of the headlong death below,—

'And " Ring, ring, thou passing-bell," still she cried,
   "i' the old chapelle ! "
       Toll slowly.
Then back-toppling, crashing back—a dead weight
   flung out to wrack,
Horse and riders overfell.'

Tennyson had revived the refrain, and both in these ballads and some of her later poems, Mrs. Browning makes most effective use of it. ' The nightingales, the nightingales,' ' Pan, Pan is dead,' ' And now my spinning is all done,' ' At last we're tired, my heart and I,' carry their own wistful tale.

The little *Romance of the Swan* is a well-known favourite ; and here too we may notice the poem which first made Miss Barrett's fame, *Lady Geraldine's Courtship*. Her low-born, poet-hero, Bertram, has been called, not without justice, a dreadful prig, ' a libel upon the whole race of poets ; ' but her heroine, her verse, and her remarkable and at that time courageous avowal of democratic convictions, were enough to win quick reputation for the poetess.

Then there are the many poems having classical subjects for their motives, of which perhaps *The Dead Pan* is the most striking, and *A Musical Instrument* the most perfect. The former—founded on an old legend that in the hour of Christ's agony a cry, ' Great Pan is dead,' was heard to sweep over the waves, and the oracles ceased—shows at one and the same time how great was the attraction that Greek literature held for Mrs. Browning, and the absence in herself of the Hellenic spirit.   To ' the old Hellenic tongue ' belong the

      ' Poets' songs the sweetest sung,'

and only a lover of their songs could have written—

> ' Have ye left the mountain places,
>   Oreads wild, for other tryst ?
>   Shall we see no sudden faces
>   Strike a glory through the mist ?
>   Not a sound the silence thrills
>   Of the everlasting hills :
>   Pan, Pan is dead.'

Her intimate knowledge of Greek mythology is specially
evident here, and many an unobtrusive epithet betrays her
love for it ; and this in a poem where such praise is necessarily at a minimum, for its whole object is a protest against
Schiller's lament for the lost 'gods of Hellas.'   Mrs. Browning had no trace of the tendency to exalt pagan art and
philosophy at the expense of later developments of the
human spirit under the genius of Christianity ; not only was
her living belief in the Christian faith too strong for that,
but her artistic instincts were also against it.   Like her
husband she held the highest art to be that in which

> ' More's felt than is perceived,
>   And more's perceived than can be interpreted,'
>   *Aurora Leigh,*

and therefore as the beautiful, insubstantial myths of fancy
are dispersed, she can acquiesce in gladness, and feels
Schiller's attitude of sorrow to be ' still more dishonouring
to poetry than to Christianity.'

> ' Earth outgrows the mythic fancies
>   Sung beside her in her youth,
>   And those debonair romances
>   Sound but dull beside the truth.
>   Phœbus' chariot-course is run :
>   Look up, poets, to the sun !
>   Pan, Pan is dead.'

She is even content to endanger her own work by enforcing

her doctrine in lines less poetical and more didactic than these.

Sustained freshness, clear intention, even workmanship, lift *A Musical Instrument* to a unique place among the shorter classical lyrics.   Not a word could be spared as the song changes from the havoc wrought by the god in his rough seizure of the reed—

> ' The limpid water turbidly ran,
> And the broken lilies a-dying lay,
> And the dragon-fly had fled away,
>   Ere he brought it out of the river ; '

and from his subsequent mutilation of it, to the wonder of his music, and its renovating magic—

> ' The sun on the hill forgot to die,
> And the lilies revived, and the dragon-fly
>   Came back to dream on the river.'

And here, instead of the sometimes cumbersome moral, a deeper meaning is lightly touched in with a single line— ' Making a poet out of a man '—with such felicity as to heighten instead of weighting the poetry.

In poems about children, infancy, motherhood, Mrs. Browning's tenderness and her sense of awe in the presence of the mysteries of life have free scope.

> ' A solemn thing it is to me
>   To look upon a babe that sleeps,
>   Wearing in its spirit-deeps
> The undeveloped mystery
>   Of our Adam's taint and woe,
> Which, when they developed be,
>   Will not let it slumber so ;
> Lying new in life beneath
> The shadow of the coming death,
> With that soft, low, quiet breath.'
>   *Isobel's Child.*

Little Mattie, Void in Law, A Child's Grave at Florence, Mother and Poet, overflow with the like feeling; but one's thoughts turn still more naturally to the *Song for Ragged Schools*—for the 'ragged children with bare feet,' whom the angels know the names of.

> ' Patient children—think what pain
> Makes a young child patient—ponder! '

And above all to the *Cry of the Children* oppressed in factories. 'The passion,' says the heroine of a modern novel in words the more emphatic from their contrast to her consistently light handling of every other topic, ' The passion one can feel through the wrongs of a child is something *awful.* One can feel it for any child—for all children.' [1] This is just Mrs. Browning's case; and even the slowly-worked machinery of legislation was hastened for relief of the children by the moving verses in which her great pity and indignation found vent.

> 'For all day, the wheels are droning, turning ;
>   Their wind comes in our faces,
> Till our hearts turn, our heads with pulses burning.
>   And the walls turn in their places :
> Turns the sky in the high window blank and reeling,
>   Turns the long light that drops adown the wall,
> Turn the black flies that crawl along the ceiling,
>   All are turning, all the day, and we with all.
> And all day long the iron wheels are droning,
>   And sometimes we could pray,
> "Oh, ye wheels " (breaking out in a mad moaning),
>   " Stop ! be silent for to-day ! " '

Home affection invariably calls out warmth of utterance, as in the concluding stanzas of *The Pet Name;* and here too we may notice, as allied in emotion though not in

----

[1] *Through One Administration.*

subject, the poem that has thrown yet another halo of consecration over the name of Cowper.

> ' O poets, from a maniac's tongue was poured the deathless singing !
> O Christians, at your cross of hope a hopeless hand was clinging !
> O men, this man in brotherhood your weary paths beguiling,
> Groaned inly while he taught you peace, and died while you were
>   smiling !
>
> *   *   *   *
>
> He shall be strong to sanctify the poet's high vocation,
> And bow the meekest Christian down in meeker adoration ;
> Nor ever shall he be in praise, by wise or good forsaken,
> Named softly as the household name of one whom God hath taken.'
>
> Cowper's Grave.

Her other special poem on death—*The Sleep*—has itself received a new grace of association in having been sung as the anthem at Robert Browning's funeral.

> ' O earth, so full of dreary noises !
> O men, with wailing in your voices !
> O delvéd gold, the wailers' heap !
> O strife, O curse, that o'er it fall !
> God strikes a silence through you all,
> And giveth His beloved, sleep.'

In the poems connected with her marriage we come to the very ' sermon's text.'   In *A Woman's Shortcomings* she had already lifted up a standard of what true love should be to her whom it possesses—

> ' Unless you can think when the song is done,
>   No other is soft in the rhythm ;
> Unless you can feel, when left by One
>   That all men else go with him ;
> Unless you can know, when unpraised by his breath,
>   That your beauty itself wants proving ;
> Unless you can swear, " For life, for death ! "—
>   Oh, fear to call it loving ! '

All this and far more it was to herself.   She had looked for

Death, and Love found her; and at first in her bewilderment she could scarcely realise the joy, or consent that another should take up the burden of her weary life. Two or three short poems, *Life and Love*, *A Denial*, *Inclusions*, sound like the uncertain preludings that in early days of spring herald the thrush's full-throated song; then in *Sonnets from the Portuguese* comes the clear outpouring of a living heart like Shirley Keeldar's, 'Like a shrine,—for it was holy; like snow,—for it was pure; like flame,—for it was warm; like death,—for it was strong.'

A Denial throbs with love too unselfish to own itself; too scrupulous to do other than bless—and relinquish. In *Inclusions* the scruples are giving way, overborne by a love that would take no denial. The *Sonnets*, behind the slight disguise of their title, unveil the whole intensely personal story, from the first revelation of the mystic Shape, 'Not Death, but Love,' the first resolve

> 'To live on still in love, and yet in vain,—
>   To bless thee, yet renounce thee to thy face';

to the last assured joy and avowal—

> 'I love thee freely, as men strive for Right;
> I love thee purely, as they turn from Praise.
> I love thee with the passion put to use
> In my old griefs, and with my childhood's faith.'

English poetry has only two other sonnet-sequences to count with this—Shakespeare's sonnets, and Dante Rossetti's *House of Life*. That Mrs. Browning should, at the zenith of her powers, and in the radiance of her love, have chosen this particular vehicle of expression, is a matter for all lovers of poetry to rejoice in. There could be no danger that the sonnet in her hands should be merely artificial, while the strict laws of its construction necessitated just the artistic restraint and finish from the lack of which some of her other work suffers much.   The character of these sonnets is all her own.   Aglow with light and love, it is the brightness that transfigures without hiding the deep-engraven traces of former pain, 'the rainbow gleam of smiles through tears,' to most of us so much more touching than even the beautiful, shadowless joy of untried youth.   They are full of the truest pathos, the blending of joy with an undertone of remembered sadness.

> 'As brighter ladies do not count it strange,
>   For love, to give up acres and degree,
>   I yield the grave for thy sake, and exchange
>   My near sweet view of Heaven for earth with thee.'

> 'Belovéd, dost thou love? or did I see all
>   The glory as I dreamed, and fainted when
>   Too vehement love dilated my ideal,
>   For my soul's eyes?   Will that light come again,
>   As now these tears come—falling hot and real?'

There is pathos in them such as we hear in the song of the robin among birds; in Mendelssohn's Wedding March; in the chiming of sweet-toned, consecrated bells; in that most pathetic psalm, 'Then were we like unto them that dream; then was our mouth filled with laughter and our tongue with joy. . . .   They that sow in tears shall reap in joy'; in the meeting drawn by his hand who in modern literature lays the surest finger on the deep springs of feeling, when Lady Castlewood receives back Esmond with the words of this very psalm upon her lips.

Fresh developments of vitality and power followed Mrs. Browning's marriage.   In subsequent poems her subjects become stronger, her diction purer, her verse more flexible.

She flung herself heart and soul into the great struggle for the freedom and unity of Italy, and poured out poem after poem in the cause of her adopted country. She was the last to rejoice in her own home's happiness without thought for what lay beyond its sheltering walls; all that her words—and in them lay her strength—could do, was done, and is to this day gratefully commemorated in Florence.

Casa Guidi Windows, the longest of these poems, was written in two parts with an interval of nearly three years between them, during which interval the year 1849 had brought its crushing disasters and disillusionment upon Italian patriots; naturally therefore her strain is saddened in the second part. Ten years later Italian hopes rose high again, and Mrs. Browning, with too ready confidence in the French Emperor's magnanimity, wrote *Napoleon III. in Italy*, and the rest of her *Poems before Congress*, of which *A Court Lady* has the palm.

'Happy are all free peoples, too strong to be dispossessed.
But blessed are those among nations, who dare to be strong for the rest!'

Indeed few except Mazzini foresaw how dearly the French alliance would be purchased, and to Mrs. Browning the Treaty of Villafranca came as a blow so heavy that it told severely on her health, and evidently helped to shorten her life. She died at Florence, in June 1861.

Between the two dates of revolution in Italy, Mrs. Browning had worked out and published her longest and most ambitious poem, *Aurora Leigh*. Looked at in one way, this is a novel in verse with an improbable plot, and beset with the difficulties inherent in an autobiography related by the heroine. Perhaps it is best to own the worst at once, and admit that, taken as a whole, Aurora's own criticism of her own poem would not be altogether misplaced in application to it—

> 'The range uneven, the points of sight obscure,
>   The music interrupted.'

In some parts the poetic inspiration does seem to halt a good deal, and sometimes noisy words have escaped from the control that calmer judgment would have placed upon them.   Then to make one who tells her own story produce the attractive effect upon readers that she is bound somehow to let them know she has produced upon the men and women around her, is a difficulty of the first order, and it is no great disparagement to say that Aurora scarcely overcomes it.   She does not make quite an ideal heroine.   She is either not weak enough, or not strong enough for her part in the world; too strong to become her cousin Romney's wife at once on his own terms, yet not strong enough, after her spirited refusal, either to face or silence the love and longing which for ten years onward take the zest out of her work, and the joy out of her life.   And her sadness is too much in view, too long drawn out.   One can imagine how Lucy Snowe, or still more certainly Jane Eyre, would have taken her in hand and uttered about three pungent sentences, which, if they had not made her any happier, would all at once have taught her a great deal, cut short many plainings, and assuredly have compelled her to a demeanour of less helpless self-betrayal.   For Aurora is not in the least aware how clearly she exhibits her inmost heart, not even when two or three different people have spoken out her secret before her face.   At the very last, when all is set right between the two, she still says in perfect good faith—

> 'As I live
> I should have died so, crushing in my hand
> This rose of lŏve, the wasp inside and all,
> Ignoring ever to my soul and you
> Both rose and pain.'

Her self-deception on this point is more complete than the reader can quite accept as possible. No doubt the writer's difficulty is that both Aurora's and Romney's extreme dissatisfaction with themselves, and with the partial failure of their work, *have* to be exhibited in order to point the highly characteristic moral that neither devotion to poetry, nor devotion to philanthropy, is enough in itself; both are inwardly unsatisfying and outwardly imperfect without personal love.

> 'Art symbolises heaven, but Love is God
> And makes heaven.'

But when all this is allowed, there remains much more to be said of the book's merits. Aurora is avowedly the exponent of Mrs. Browning's creed in matters of Art, and all the passages devoted to this are full of beauty and interest.

> 'Art's the witness of what Is
> Behind this show.'

> 'We stand here, we,
> If genuine artists, witnessing for God's
> Complete, consummate, undivided work.'

> 'O sorrowful great gift
> Conferred on poets, of a twofold life,
> When one life has been found enough for pain!'

A few beautiful descriptions of landscape, English and Italian, find place here; and the poet is on almost her strongest ground in her lovely drawing of Marian Erle's

motherhood and infant child.   Much interest, again, lies in
her treatment of the place and work of women, and although
Aurora leaves the position she theoretically holds to
'generalise' recklessly on feminine characteristics—com-
pelling even Romney himself, after she has at last exploded
the not very exalted estimate he originally held of a woman's
powers, to tell her—

> 'You sweep your sex
> With somewhat bitter gusts from where you live
> Above them,'

—much can be forgiven in virtue of the admirable advice
she presses home.

> 'A woman cannot do the thing she ought,
> Which means whatever perfect thing she can,
> In life, in art, in science, but she fears
> To let the perfect action take her part,
> And rest there : she must prove what she can do
> Before she does it, prate of woman's rights,
> Of woman's mission, woman's function, till
> The men (who are prating too on their side) cry,
> "A woman's function plainly is . . . to talk."
> Poor souls, they are very reasonably vexed ;
> They cannot hear each other talk.
>
>   *   *   *   *
>
> 'By speaking we prove only we can speak,
> Which he, the man here, never doubted.   What
> He doubts is, whether we can *do* the thing
> With decent grace we've not yet done at all.
> Now, do it ; bring your statue,—you have room !
>
>   *   *   *   *
>
> 'There's no need to speak ;
> The universe shall henceforth speak for you,
> And witness, "She who did this thing, was born
> To do it,—claims her license in her work."'

The satirical touches here are also very characteristic; such
light shafts fly about in all directions.

'The poor-club exercised her Christian gifts
Of knitting stockings, stitching petticoats,
Because we are of one flesh, after all,
And need one flannel (with a proper sense
Of difference in the quality).'—BK. I.

'She thanked God and sighed,
(Some people always sigh in thanking God).'—BK. I.

'Because a lord
Is still more potent than a poetess
With any extreme republican.'—BK. V.

'He sets his virtues on so raised a shelf,
To keep them at the grand millennial height,
He has to mount a stool to get at them ;
And, meantime, lives on quite the common way,
With everybody's morals.'—BK. V.

But after all, we turn back to a few short lyrics, *The Cry of the Children, Cowper's Grave, A Musical Instrument,* and above all to the unmatched *Sonnets from the Portuguese,* for our keenest enjoyment of Mrs. Browning's tenderness, pathos, and the fine insight of a strong and guileless spirit.

IV.

ARTHUR HUGH CLOUGH.
MATTHEW ARNOLD.

'Perplext in faith, but pure in deeds.'
In Memoriam.
'The one great thing is to have a life of one's own.'
Lacordaire.

OF the two poets closely linked in friendship, associations,
and an intellectual tendency of thought which both have
represented in poetry, the work of the elder is still comparatively little known—far less than it deserves to be—in spite
of the high estimation of it repeatedly expressed by those
best able to judge of its merits. The few who do know and
care, are too much inclined to take it for granted that Clough
can only be valued, as they say, by 'highly educated and
meditative thinkers,' and to give up at the outset any
effort to make his poetry more widely known. It has
been said again and again that his poetry never will be
popular; and more, that it *cannot* be. It may be so ; yet
let us hope that the rapidly growing influence of the
Universities will open up a knowledge of their traditions
and ways to ever-widening circles of students, and with it
the power to enter into certain enjoyments whose finest
flavour is reserved for the sons and friends of Oxford.

Meantime lovers of Clough's poetry are occasionally to be
met with in such unexpected places as to suggest that
imperfect opportunities have had as much or more than
indifference to do with the blank ignorance of him in
others.   It is generally to be noticed, too, that the well-
worn condition of the volume of Clough's poems speaks
eloquently to the tenacious hold the contents have taken of
its happy owner.   'A poet does not deserve the name,' it
has been said, 'who would not rather be read a thousand
times by one man than a single time by a thousand;' and
tried by that test, Clough is a poet indeed.

Arthur Hugh Clough was born in 1819 at Liverpool, but
most of his childhood was spent in America with the rest
of his family.   At nine years old he was sent back to
England, to a school at Chester; and a year later he was
entered at Rugby, then under the headmastership of Dr.
Arnold.   His career at school was brilliant; he was one of
Dr. Arnold's best and favourite pupils, and also one of those
most deeply impressed by the fervour of Arnold's religious
life and belief.   Leaving Rugby for Oxford, he came into
immediate contact with Newman, whose influence in Oxford
was then at its strongest, and Clough afterwards described
himself as having been for two years ' like a straw drawn up
the draught of a chimney.'   The consequence of passing in
this way from the influence of one strong leader to that of
another, upon a mind like Clough's—thoughtful, impression-
able, and before all things absolutely sincere—was to force
him very early to face and examine the most difficult
questions of life that can be put before any thinker.   The
keen logic of Newman destroyed in him the faith of Arnold,
yet he could not for long bring himself to accept the groundwork of assumptions demanded by the faith of Newman.

He was thrown into a state of uncertainty best described in his own words, which show the courage of his character as well as the trouble of his mind.

'Here am I yet, another twelvemonth spent,
*   *   *   *
'Sails rent,
And rudder broken, reason impotent,
Affections all unfixed ; so forth I fare
On the mid seas unheedingly, so dare
To do and to be done by, well content.'[1]

The transition from the creed of Arnold through Tract-arianism to inability to accept any dogmatic creed at all, occupied several years. In the meantime, he had, after taking his degree, been appointed a Fellow and Tutor of Oriel College, a position which, besides being highly honour-able, gave him congenial work as a lecturer. But it assumed an adherence to religious beliefs which became by degrees impossible to him, and nothing shows more plainly his perfect unworldliness and sincerity than the fact that as soon as he realised this, he resigned both tutorship and fellowship, leaving himself for the time without any means of livelihood, at a moment, too, when there were serious calls upon him from family and friends for help, always given to the utmost of his power. The reason of his resignation

[1] It is a curious and highly suggestive fact that two poets whose mental attitude in religious matters was so widely different as that of Cowper and Clough should have used the same image and nearly the same words to describe it. Compare with the above lines these from Cowper's poem *On the Receipt of my Mother's Picture*—

'Me howling blasts drive devious, tempest-toss'd,
Sails ripp'd, seams opening wide, and compass lost ;
And day by day some current's thwarting force
Sets me more distant from a prosperous course.'

stood in the way of his obtaining other work suited to him ; and when he did gain an appointment to the headship of an unsectarian Hall in London, he passed through a dreary time of isolation and cold treatment. He had, however, the great satisfaction of friendships made with first Emerson, and then Carlyle. In 1852 he went to America, intending to settle there ; but in less than a year was brought back again by the offer of an Examinership in the Education Office, which post he held till his death. His marriage took place in 1854, and the next two years were filled for him with steady official work, happy domestic life, and with many interests of a social and public kind, especially that in the work of his relative, Miss Florence Nightingale. Then, unhappily, his health gave way ; travelling to restore it was unsuccessful, and in November 1861 he died at Florence, at the early age of forty-two, leaving England the poorer by a poet whose vocation was only half fulfilled.

For during these years of varied work, and often trying experiences, it was only now and then that he had at once both the peaceful leisure and the stimulus that were necessary for poetry-writing to his sensitive nature ; and though the vigorous poems he has left are themselves of great value, they contain the promise of something greater, if he had lived to execute it.

The same characteristics mark Clough's poetry as may be gathered from even so short a sketch as this of his life,— fearlessness, honesty, a strong interest, almost preoccupation, with religious questions, and after them with social problems ; determination not to take things for granted, but to scrutinise them for himself ; no hasty jumping at conclusions, but much patient waiting and consideration of conflicting views. They are stamped too with his high-toned unselfishness, and bear the marks of his sensitiveness. In addition there is to many readers a peculiar attractiveness about his versification ; not always faultless, nor, except in some of the lyrics, very musical, but with a unique vigour and freshness of its own.   It may sound like two-edged praise to say that persons usually indifferent to poetry have been known to find themselves unexpectedly enjoying his ; but the wrong edge is turned by adding—which is also true —that the attraction is by no means confined to readers whose poetic sensibilities are not over-acute.

Clough's longest poem, the *Bothie of Tober-na-Vuolich*, was written soon after he quitted Oxford, and sets forth with much breezy life and vigour, in a perfectly original form, the views of life then fermenting in the minds of young men stirred by the thousand anomalies around them —the contradictions between the real and ideal.   A 'reading party' of Oxford men spend the long vacation in Scotland under charge of a tutor—

> 'the grave man, nicknamed Adam,
> White-tied, clerical, silent, with antique square-cut waistcoat,
> Formal, unchanged, of black cloth, but with sense and feeling beneath it ;
> Skilful in Ethics and Logic, in Pindar and Poets unrivalled ;
> *Shady* in Latin, said Lindsay, but *topping* in Plays and Aldrich.'

Each of the party has his own clearly-marked character, but the most conspicuous among them is—

> 'Philip Hewson a poet,
> Hewson a radical hot, hating lords and scorning ladies,'

and the interest of the poem turns on his discussions with Adam of the problems of rank and station, love, marriage, education, riches, poverty, and a hundred other matters ;

and on his captivation successively, now in spite of and now according to his theories, by the cottage-girl Katie, the high-bred Lady Maria, and finally by sweet Elspie Mackaye, the Highlander's daughter, as good and sensible as she is pretty. With their marriage and emigration to New Zealand the poem ends.

Philip's fervid eloquence, Adam's deliberate yet ready replies, dictated by moderating wisdom, the shrewd and lively comments thrown in by others of the party, especially the 'cheery, cigar-loving Lindsay,' nicknamed the Piper, keep the debates astir with unflagging animation and humour. Here are a few lines from a burst of discussion on the ideal relation between men and women. Philip, with the bit in his teeth, has been declaiming at great length (much to the Piper's wrath, who could scarcely get in a word of dissent) on the superior charms of women occupied in household or harder work, over those of fine ladies with men

> 'Dangling beside them, and turning the leaves on the dreary piano,
> Offering unneeded arms, and performing dull farces of escort.'

Real goodness, answers Adam, is independent of either position, and possible in both.

> 'Ah, you have much to learn ; we can't know all things at twenty.
> Partly you rest on truth, old truth, the duty of Duty ;
> Partly on error, you long for equality.
>   Ay, cried the Piper.
> That's what it is, that confounded *égalité*, French manufacture ;
> He is the same as the Chartist who spoke at a meeting in Ireland,
> *What, and is not one man, fellow-man, as good as another ?*
> *Faith*, replied Pat, *and a deal better too !*
>   So rattled the Piper.'

Later on a different element comes into the poem. Here

is Elspie's very original reception of Philip's agitated
question—

        ' Well, she answered,
And she was silent some time, and blushed all over, and answered
Quietly, after her fashion, still knitting, Maybe, I think of it,
Though I don't know that I did : and she paused again ; but it
   may be,
Yes—I don't know, Mr. Philip—but only it feels to me strangely,
Like to the high new bridge, they used to build at, below there,
Over the burn and glen on the road. You don't understand me ;
But I keep saying in my mind—this long time slowly with trouble
I have been building myself up, up, and toilfully raising,
Just like as if the bridge were to do it itself without masons,
Painfully getting myself upraised, one stone on another,
All one side, I mean ; and now I see on the other
Just such another fabric uprising, better and stronger,
Close to me, coming to join me ; and then I sometimes fancy—
Sometimes I find myself dreaming at nights about arches and bridges—
Sometimes I dream of a great invisible hand coming down, and
Dropping the great key-stone in the middle : there in my dreaming,
There I felt the great key-stone coming in, and through it
Feel the other part, all the other stones of the archway,
Joined into mine with a strange, happy sense of completeness. But,
   dear me,
This is confusion and nonsense. I mix all the things I can think of,
And you won't understand, Mr. Philip.'

Philip's last discussion with Adam (by letter, after months
of interval) is as characteristic as his first. He would have
each do only ' the thing we are meant for,' perfectly regard-
less of social station ; and Adam replies—

' When the armies are set in array and the battle beginning,
  Is it well that the soldier whose post is far to the leftward
  Say, I will go to the right, it is there I shall do best service ?
  There is a great Field-Marshal, my friend, who arrays our battalions ;
  Let us to Providence trust, and abide and work in our stations.
   This was the final retort from the eager, impetuous Philip.

I am sorry to say your Providence puzzles me sadly ;
Children of Circumstance are we to be? you answer, On no wise !
Where does Circumstance end, and Providence, where begins it?
What are we to resist, and what are we to be friends with?'

Nevertheless there is a ring of satisfaction in the close not
often to be met with in these poems. And the graver parts
of the *Bothie* are set in delightfully bright descriptions of
Scottish hills and glens, fresh with the very breezes of the
Highlands.

If Philip Hewson's intellectual conclusions were far from
settled, at least his practical course became clear; but in
the next long poem, the *Amours de Voyage*, not so much
certainty as this is attained. Clough prefixed to this a
motto from a French novel, 'He doubted everything, even
love.' The hero, Mr. Claude, is overtaken in Rome by the
French siege of the city in 1849. He makes acquaintance
with a family of English visitors, and is, as any one but
himself would say, in love with one of the daughters. For
his own part he cannot make up his mind whether he is
in love or not, and is nervously afraid of giving himself
up to it—

'I do not like being moved ; for the will is excited ; and action
Is a most dangerous thing ; I tremble for something factitious,
Some malpractice of heart and illegitimate process ;
We are so prone to these things with our terrible notions of duty.'

He is equally uncertain on most other points ; is not sure
whether he likes Rome or not, remains curiously neutral
in the midst of Italian enthusiasm under Mazzini, hesitates
whether to go or stay, speak or keep silence. He allows
the young lady to leave Rome, and then sets off on a very
unskilfully-managed pursuit, which is in the end a failure ;
whereupon he consoles himself by reflecting—

'After all, do I know that I really cared so about her?
*   *   *   *
After all, perhaps there was something factitious about it ;
I have had pain, it is true ; I have wept, and so have the actors.'

The interest here lies in the highly skilful delineation of
this fastidious, doubtful, hesitating mind, obviously a most
difficult task.   It contains also many clever character-
touches, such as those shown in the different effects produced
by the same sights on the sightseers.   When the siege has
begun Mr. Claude admits that it is 'an experience, that,
among others!' to have a man killed before his eyes (by
the way, he is not sure that he saw it—could not declare
in court that he did; but he saw something in a place
where they said a man was killed); but to Georgina
Trevellyn and her friends, less startling experiences become
'the fearful scenes we have witnessed.'   The quiet irony
of drawing such a figure as Mr. Claude, with all his dread of
action, against the background of Garibaldi's and Mazzini's
deeds in that year of heroic strain, enhances the effect, and
is emphasised—still quietly—in the epilogue—

'I was writ in a Roman chamber,
When from Janiculan heights thundered the cannon of France.'

These two poems are further remarkable as being among
the very few English poems successfully written in hexameters.   The fact that the measurement of feet in classical
poetry depends on the *length*, and not, as in English, on
the *accent* of syllables, makes it very hard to obtain the
peculiar and characteristic *lilt* of hexameters in English
verse; and though many attempts have been made—Longfellow's *Evangeline* being the best known—hardly any have
succeeded, and indeed some critics say that success is in

the nature of things impossible. But others allow that Clough's *Bothie* and Kingsley's *Andromeda* are in the main correct as well as spirited.

The tales of *Mari Magno*, related to each other on shipboard by a little group of fellow-voyagers crossing the Atlantic, are broader and simpler than the last subtle study; but in them, too, Clough's sympathetic knowledge of the self-questioning spirit shows itself—

> 'A touch
> Of something introspective overmuch.
> With all his eager notions still there went
> A self-correcting and ascetic bent,
> That from the obvious good still led astray,
> And set him travelling on the longest way.'

Dipsychus ('having two minds') is devoted to the struggle undergone by a sensitive, thoughtful, conscientious mind drawn in two opposite directions by the aspirations of a noble nature on the one hand, and promptings to acquiescence in common standards of morality and action on the other. The almost morbidly sensitive organisation of Dipsychus is brought out not only in the entanglement of doubts and questionings to which it lays him open, but in the effect upon him of callous worldliness, or of sights common enough in Venice, and too commonly disregarded.

> 'Lo, scarce come forth,
> Some vagrant miscreant meets, and with a look
> Transmutes me his, and for a whole sick day
> Lepers me.'

Or again in cravings stifled back upon themselves in pessimism too radically restless to find real calm in its appeal to stoical resignation.

> ' Where are the great, whom thou would'st wish to praise thee?
> Where are the pure, whom thou would'st choose to love thee?
> Where are the brave to stand supreme above thee,
> Whose high commands would cheer, whose chidings raise thee?
>   Seek, seeker, in thyself; submit to find
>   In the stones, bread, and life in the blank mind.'

The spirit who debates with Dipsychus, and answers eagerly to his ejaculated 'Mephistopheles!' presents a contrast to him at every point; he is the shallow, calculating exponent of pure worldliness, as clever as he is unscrupulous. His mocking gibes often carry the sting of partial truth under their flippancy—

> ' Well now, it's anything but clear
> What is the tone that's taken here:
> What is your logic? What's your theology?
> Is it, or is it not, neology?
> That's a great fault; you're this and that,
> And here and there, and nothing flat.'

His cynical worldliness is sometimes too frankly avowed even for worldlings, sometimes such a precise rendering of common notions as would entrap others besides the speaker in the prose epilogue into the confession of admitting, 'Not that he didn't say much which, if only it hadn't been for the way he said it, and that it was he who said it, would have been sensible enough.'

The dialogue between these two, as suggested by their surroundings, proceeds through many turns and winds, becoming rather too obscure in the latter part of the poem, till its not very definite issue is reached, when the spirit boasts, though with ill-disguised misgivings—

> ' No matter, no matter, the bargain's made,
> And I, for my part, will not be afraid;'

and Dipsychus, calling him

> 'The Power of this World ! hateful unto God,'

repels him with the more assured rejoinder.

> 'Yet in all these things we—'tis Scripture too—
> Are more than conquerors, even over you.'

One 'Gondola Song' is noticeable as almost the smoothest and most musical bit of writing in all Clough's verse.

> 'How light we go, how softly ! Ah,
> Were life but as the gondola !'

Clough is unsparingly severe upon hollow pretences, compliance with form for form's sake, sordid self-interest masked under the guise of respectability, and his impatience with them sometimes finds expression in stinging satire, as when he writes his poem, on *Duty*—

> 'Duty—'tis to take on trust
> What things are good and right and just ;
> And whether indeed they be or be not,
> Try not, test not, feel not, see not ;'

or when, as we have just seen, he puts the phrases of a debased yet current morality into the mouth of the Spirit in *Dipsychus*, or again gives in *The Latest Decalogue* a translation of the Ten Commandments as understood and practised in certain walks of modern life.

> 'Honour thy parents ; that is, all
> From whom advancement may befall.
>   * * *
> Thou shalt not steal ; an empty feat,
> When it's so lucrative to cheat.
>   * * *
> Thou shalt not covet, but tradition
> Approves all forms of competition.'

For utterances such as these Clough has been called cynical,
just as Thackeray is called cynical by those who do not
discern between the pen that exposes to chastise and, if it
may be, cure, and the pen that exposes in bravado or out of
a kind of callous pleasure in exposure.

In his own person Clough treats the same topics as those
of the *Bothie* and *Dipsychus* in a number of short and often
very beautiful lyrics, which are perhaps the most permanently
valuable part of his work.   One of the most striking is
Easter Day (*Naples* 1849), with its mournful burden—

> 'Christ is not risen, no—
> He lies and moulders low ;
> Christ is not risen ! '

to which an early reference in *Dipsychus* supplies a key in
the words—

> 'Ah ! and I think at Venice
> Christ is not risen either.'

This is one of several poems in which his interweaving of
well-known phrases sacred to religion has a singular fascination.   Needless to say, nothing could be more dangerous to
imitate ; but somehow a deeper reverence seems to breathe
from Clough's denials than many people can manage to
express in their assertions of faith.

> 'Ashes to ashes, dust to dust ;
> As of the unjust, also of the just—
> Yea, of that just One too !
> This is the one sad Gospel that is true—
> Christ is not risen !
>   *   *   *
> 'One look, and then depart,
> Ye holy and ye humble men of heart ;
> And ye ! ye ministers and stewards of a Word
> Which ye would preach, because another heard—

> Ye worshippers of that ye do not know,
>   Take these things hence and go :—
>   He is not risen !
>
> *   *   *
>
> ' Let us go hence and think upon these things
>   In silence, which is best.'

Sometimes these lyrics ring with the key-note of high
courage—' Hope evermore and believe, O man !' sometimes
the stress of life brings in a sadder tone, still brave, as in
the exquisite *Qua cursum Ventus,* that describes the unwilling
estrangement of friends under the image of ships whose
courses have parted unknown to each other in the darkness—

> ' To veer, how vain !   On, onward strain,
>   Brave barks !   In light, in darkness too,
> Through winds and tides one compass guides—
>   To that and your own selves, be true.
>
> *   *   *   *
>
> One port, methought, alike they sought,
>   One purpose hold where'er they fare—
> O bounding breeze, O rushing seas !
>   At last, at last, unite them there ! '

Equal if not greater confidence breathes through the quiet
lines of *We'll meet again upon some future day*—

> ' When we have proved, each on his course alone,
>   The wider world, and learnt what's now unknown,
>   Have made life clear, and worked out each a way,
>   We'll meet again—we shall have much to say.'

Often, as in *The Shadow, The Questioning Spirit, Bethesda,*
there is a wistful sigh of regret for vanished certainties,
softening the steadfast—almost *trustful*—acceptance of
uncertainty.

> ' And taking up the word around, above, below,
>   Some querulously high, some softly, sadly low,

We know not, sang they all, nor ever need we know !
We know not, sang they, what avails to know ?

＊　　＊　　＊　　＊　　＊　　＊

I also know not and I need not know,
Only with questionings pass I to and fro,
Perplexing these that sleep, and in their folly
Imbreeding doubt and sceptic melancholy ;
Till that, their dreams deserting, they with me
Come all to this true ignorance and thee.'

The Questioning Spirit.

It has been said of Clough that he was one of those who
'will not fall into place in the ordinary intellectual world
anyhow. If you offer them any known religion, they "won't
have that ;" if you offer them no religion, they will not have
that either; if you ask them to accept a new and as yet
unrecognised religion, they altogether refuse to do so.' [1]
And we have only to look in order to see that this does
truthfully describe the position of most of the ' Religious
Poems.' Clough distrusts the 'new lights' even more than
the old, as *The New Sinai* bears witness. ' Ah, yet consider
it again,' he says elsewhere of the old faith scornfully
rejected—

' " Old things need not be therefore true,"
O brother men, nor yet the new ;
Ah ! still awhile the old thought retain,
And yet consider it again !'

The upshot of his own reflections is oftenest suspension of
judgment; he tends on the whole—

' To pace the sad confusion through,
And say :— It doth not yet appear
What we shall be, what we are here.'

Through a Glass Darkly.

---

[1] Bagehot, *Literary Studies*, vol. ii.

There are, however, two or three poems of delicate power
and beauty, especially *Qui laborat, orat*, and one beginning—

> ' O Thou whose image in the shrine
>   Of human spirits dwells divine,'

in which there is indicated a faith too shadowy to satisfy the
robust theologian, too assured to please the secularist, a
faith that makes Clough, like Emerson, 'the friend and
aider of those who would live in the spirit.'   He represents
the men and women who have grown up in the teachings of
some strict, clearly-defined religious faith, and on leaving
its bounds, have carried with them all the earnestness it has
taught into inquiries searching indeed, but pure from the
least taint of flippancy or irreverence.   Whether happy or
not, such an attitude held by one absolutely true to his
convictions or his doubts is noble, and may be helpful, as
Clough has made it.   We find in his poems much uncertainty, but no despair ; and gladly we recognise the
accents of victory, subdued though their tone may be, in the
last poem he ever wrote—

> ' Say not, the struggle nought availeth,
>   The labour and the wounds are vain,
> The enemy faints not, nor faileth,
>   And as things have been they remain.

> ' If hopes were dupes, fears may be liars ;
>   It may be, in yon smoke concealed,
> Your comrades chase e'en now the fliers,
>   And, but for you, possess the field.

> ' For while the tired waves, vainly breaking,
>   Seem here no painful inch to gain,
> Far back, through creeks and inlets making,
>   Comes silent, flooding in, the main ;

' And not by eastern windows only,
    When daylight comes, comes in the light,
In front, the sun climbs slow, how slowly,
    But westward, look, the land is bright.'

LIKE his friend Clough, Matthew Arnold is essentially the poet of his own time, of *our* time; and like him too, his thoughts are much occupied with our contending intellectual and religious ideas, the illogical confusions of men's minds, and the harassing nature of their practice.

> ' This tract which the river of Time
>   Now flows through with us, is the plain.
>   Gone is the calm of its earlier shore.
>   Border'd by cities and hoarse
>   With a thousand cries is its stream.
>   And we on its breast, our minds
>   Are confused as the cries which we hear,
>   Changing and shot as the sights which we see.'
>   *The Future.*

But the rare poems which, though only a part, are perhaps the best part of his legacy to literature, are the outcome of a very different poetic genius from Clough's; less spontaneous and robust, they are more musical, and far more finished in workmanship, as befits artistic work from the hand of the apostle of Culture. Their range is not very wide; their whole number is not very large; they are not like the work of a man whose life is given up to poetry, who looks at everything in the light of his poet's mind, and brings every kind of experience into his pages. But within their own range poems so lucid, so finely thoughtful, so choice in word and phrase, bear the hall-mark of fine distinction. Matthew Arnold among poets stands like Sir Philip Sidney among knights; less powerful than some, his record of achievements shorter and less varied, but lifted by their perfection of graceful and gracious performance into the front rank of the finest spirits of his day.

Many and potent influences went to the fashioning of this poet. Both by inheritance and cultivation, certain didactic tendencies belong to him; the son of Dr. Arnold, the disciple of Goethe and Wordsworth, might have said with as much truth as any of the three, 'I meant to teach you something.' To his saturation in Greek culture may be traced the form and style of his poems, their carefully disciplined restraint, their chastened beauty of language. With Goethe he discerns the purposeless fret and weariness in latter-day stress of hurrying life; after Wordsworth he turns to Nature for anodyne. But all influences were fused in him, and moulded into a new development of original and high-wrought beauty—himself.

In early days Matthew Arnold originated a theory that the function of poetry lies only in the field of action; and held to it so firmly that for a time he actually withdrew *Empedocles on Etna* because, as he said, a situation in which 'everything was to be endured, nothing to be done,' ought not to be chosen as the subject of a poem. But his own tendencies were too strong for his theories, and happily too strong also to permit the barrier of a mistaken theory to stand permanently in the way. Essentially reflective, and somewhat didactic by nature, holding always a little aloof from the world he watched with keen-sighted eyes, more cultivated than spontaneous as a poet, it was impossible for his poetry of action to touch so high a level as his meditative lyrics. *Merope*, his drama in the Greek style, counts as his least successful effort, correct but tame, and wanting in fire. *Empedocles on Etna*, though cast in dramatic form, is, as its author said, not a poem of action, but owes its chief interest to the philosophic musings of Empedocles, and its chief beauty to the lyrical songs of the flute-player Callicles. A poem in which nearly all the speech is soliloquy, and the entire action consists in the gradual ascent of a volcanic mountain, a long pause on its summit occupied with painful meditation, and a final plunge into its crater, has indeed but scant claim to the title of a drama; and it has been pointed out that even this climax is at variance with what has gone before, but not led up to it. For instead of rendering the thoughts likely to have filled the mind of the real Empedocles, in despair at the decay of true philosophy before his advancing antagonists the Sophists, Arnold has in fact clothed in this classical dress his own arraignment of human life; and further, has imbued his philosopher with his own steady determination against yielding to despair, so that the closing suicide does not come as the logical conclusion of the thinker's reasoning, but simply betrays a failure of courage, and leaves an impression that, at any rate so far as he himself is concerned, his discourse has proved itself 'a tale of little meaning, though the words are strong.'

The longer narrative poems, again, though stronger than *Merope*, are somehow wanting in force on the whole, in spite of the many beautiful passages they contain. This is especially the case with *Baldur Dead*, a treatment of the Scandinavian myth involving, like the *Odyssey*, *A Journey to the Dead*, and executed on Homeric lines, but not with Homeric life. Even in *Sohrab and Rustum* the narrative hardly seems swift enough, passionate enough, to make an event so tragic as the death of the warrior-son by the hand of his unwitting warrior-father quite so impressive as it ought to be. But the beautiful similes and stately blank verse are a joy in themselves; and the poem closes with one of Arnold's most characteristic bits of natural description, at once soothing and suggestive.

> 'But the majestic river floated on,
> Out of the mist and hum of that low land,
> Into the frosty starlight, and there moved,
> Rejoicing, through the hush'd Chorasmian waste,
> Under the solitary moon ;—he flow'd
> Right for the polar star, past Orgungè,
> Brimming and bright and large ; then sands begin
> To hem his watery march, and dam his streams,
> And split his currents ; that for many a league
> The shorn and parcell'd Oxus strains along
> Through beds of sand and matted rushy isles—
> Oxus, forgetting the bright speed he had
> In his high mountain-cradle in Pamere,
> A foil'd circuitous wanderer—till at last
> The long'd-for dash of waves is heard, and wide
> His luminous home of waters opens, bright
> And tranquil, from whose floor the new-bathed stars
> Emerge, and shine upon the Aral sea.'

Tristram and Iseult tells freshly the rather complicated story of one of the Arthurian legends; here too the principal charm is to be found in detached passages, such as the description of the sleeping children, or that of the chamber of death where Queen Iseult kneels by Sir Tristram's bedside, the two—

> 'Cold, cold as those who lived and loved
> A thousand years ago.'

Or again that of Iseult the wife, 'the young surviving Iseult,' in after days—

> 'Joy has not found her yet, nor ever will—
> Is it this thought which makes her mien so still,

Her features so fatigued, her eyes, though sweet,
So sunk, so rarely lifted save to meet
Her children's? She moves slow ; her voice alone
Hath yet an infantine and silver tone,
But even that comes languidly ; in truth
She seems one dying in a mask of youth.'

But one of the shorter narrative poems, *The Sick King
in Bokara,* has, with extreme simplicity of action, all the
unity and quiet vigour that we miss in these. Calmly yet
graphically the whole case is related—the story of a remorseful Moolah, who in the fierce heat and drought,
having hidden away a little can of water for his own use
and found it empty, had, in his thirst and fever, cursed the
drinkers, among whom was his mother; and who *would*
expiate his sin by invoking the vengeance of the broken law.
The young King's pitying reluctance to take the forfeited life ;
his futile attempts to evade giving sentence, or to nullify its
execution ; his wondering rebellion against bounds to his
own merciful will so unexpected and sternly impassable ;
the aged Vizier's grave reproof of the King's hesitation and
weak tenderness towards one neither friend nor akin to him ;
his own fatalistic acquiescence in limitations imposed by
law and the conditions of social life,—follow each other
in bright, still beauty of verse ; and the poem maintains
throughout a wonderful tone of Oriental dignity, the cere-
monious patience in speech and act, combined with un-
yielding enforcement of the demands of a long-established
order.   In the end the young King's lesson is learnt once
for all.

'But hear ye this, ye sons of men !
They that bear rule and are obey'd,
Unto a rule more strong than theirs
Are in their turn obedient made.

*   *   *   *

'Thou wast a sinner, thou poor man!
Thou wast athirst; and didst not see,
That, though we take what we desire,
We must not snatch it eagerly.

'And I have meat and drink at will,
And rooms of treasures, not a few.
But I am sick, nor heed I these;
And what I would, I cannot do.'

The Forsaken Merman (more widely known than most of Arnold's poems from having been included in volumes of miscellaneous selections) is hardly a narrative poem at all, but 'the clear cry of a creature astray in the world, wild and gentle and mournful,' the pitiful, strange wonder and yearning of unsatisfied love in the soulless one fronted by mysterious claims of religion over the loved one's soul.

But the finest beauty and strength of Arnold's poetry lies casketed in the lyrics; it is in them that we have at its clearest his own personal 'criticism of life,' which gives the special tone and value to his work. He was, as we know, profoundly influenced by Greek poets and thinkers; among them he speaks more particularly of Homer, Epictetus, and above all Sophocles, he whom

'Business could not make dull, nor passion wild;
Who saw life steadily, and saw it whole.'

A similar mighty power of 'wide and luminous view' drew him to the feet of Goethe among modern philosophers, whose influence he repeatedly analyses and acknowledges.

'Physician of the iron age,
Goethe has done his pilgrimage.
He took the suffering human race,
He read each wound, each weakness clear;
And struck his finger on the place,
And said: *Thou ailest here, and here!*'
                              Memorial Verses.

> ' And Goethe's course few sons of men
>   May think to emulate.

> ' For he pursued a lonely road,
>   His eyes on Nature's plan ;
> Neither made man too much a God,
>   Nor God too much a man.

> ' Strong was he with a spirit free
>   From mists, and sane, and clear ;
> Clearer, how much ! than ours—yet we
>   Have a worse course to steer.'—*Obermann.*

And when Arnold turns to gaze for himself on the scene
around him, it is to see and pronounce upon the worst
flaws in modern life, its ceaseless bustle, noise, unrest,
its conflict of dim and undirected aims.

> ' What is the course of the life
>   Of mortal men on the earth?—
> Most men eddy about
> Here and there—eat and drink,
> Chatter and love and hate,
> Gather and squander, are raised
> Aloft, are hurled in the dust,
> Striving blindly, achieving
> Nothing ; and then they die—
> Perish ;—and no one asks
> Who or what they have been,
> More than he asks what waves,
> In the moonlit solitudes wild
> Of the midmost Ocean, have swell'd,
> Foam'd for a moment, and gone.'—*Rugby Chapel.*

And again,

> —' Most men in a brazen prison live,
> Where, in the sun's hot eye,
> With heads bent o'er their toil, they languidly
> Their lives to some unmeaning taskwork give,
> Dreaming of nought beyond their prison-wall.

And as, year after year,
Fresh products of their barren labour fall
From their tired hands, and rest
Never yet comes more near,
Gloom settles slowly down over their breast;
And while they try to stem
The waves of mournful thought by which they are pressed,
Death in their prison reaches them,
Unfreed, having seen nothing, still unblest.'
A Summer Night.

And again,

'In cities should we English lie,
    Where cries are rising ever new,
And men's incessant stream goes by—
    We who pursue

'Our business with unslackening stride,
    Traverse in troops, with care-fill'd breast,
The soft Mediterranean side,
    The Nile, the East.

'And see all sights from pole to pole,
    And glance, and nod, and bustle by;
And never once possess our soul
    Before we die.'—*A Southern Night.*

But this is not all; if it were we might be tempted to say
as he himself says of Heine's bitter satires—

'We know all this, we know!
Cam'st thou from heaven, O child
Of light! but this to declare?
Alas, to help us forget
Such barren knowledge awhile,
God gave the poet his song!'

He sees, as he thinks, the old faiths disproved; for him
they are irrecoverably passed away; death looms up for
him as the absolute end—

'Stern law of every mortal lot!
Which man, proud man, finds hard to bear,
And builds himself I know not what
Of second life I know not where.'—*Geist's Grave*.

But the loss gives him neither scorn nor joy; it fills him
with almost unmixed pain, sadness, regret, and wrings out
the low 'Virgilian cry, the sense of tears in mortal things'
that sobs in undertone through his tranquil verse.

'Listen! you hear the grating roar
Of pebbles which the waves draw back and fling,
At their return, up the high strand,
Begin, and cease, and then again begin,
With tremulous cadence slow, and bring
The eternal note of sadness in.'—*Dover Beach*.

Sophocles heard in it the turbid ebb and flow of human
misery, Arnold hears in it 'the melancholy, long, with-
drawing roar' of the Sea of Faith once so full and bright.
He craves for light, peace, certitude, with an almost hopeless longing; but yet never suffers despondency to sink
into despair. It is resisted, held at bay. He bids the
unspeakable yearning of man's heart for joy and assurance
and fuller scope 'not fly to dreams but moderate desire,'
bids it 'nurse no extravagant hope' whose disappointment
leads to despair, but be temperate in all things. Perhaps
the influence of Epictetus has had to do with his attitude
of softened Stoicism; possibly the many phrases he appro-
priates from the language of religion to the service of
culture carry their old associations with them; certain it is
that his words often kindle the hope and brace the will,
just when what he has to say might be expected to ex-
tinguish the one and relax the other; and some who have
better hopes than his for the truth and vitality of their faith

may gain from him a new sense of its beauty, its constraining power, its sacredness.   We feel this—and cannot but
feel it—in *Progress*, in *Morality*, in the sonnet on *Immortality*, and in many another poem less hopeful than these;
we feel it as he speaks of the freedmen of the world—

> 'The Children of the Second Birth,
>   Whom the world could not tame
>
>   *   *   *   *
>
> 'Christian and pagan, king and slave,
>   Soldier and anchorite,
> Distinctions we esteem so grave,
>   Are nothing in their sight.
>
> 'They do not ask, who pined unseen,
>   Who was on action hurl'd,
> Whose one bond is, that all have been
>   Unspotted by the world.'—*Obermann*.

But the refuge to which Arnold consciously turns, the
inspiration to patience and endurance that he consciously
seeks, are alike to be found in the sanctuary of Nature.
Weary of himself, wearier of life 'with its sick hurry, its
divided aims,' he appeals to sea and stars—

> 'Ye who from my childhood up have calm'd me,
>   Calm me, ah, compose me to the end!'—*Self-Dependence*.

He calls himself, and is called in this respect, the disciple
of Wordsworth, and so he is; yet his way of resorting to
Nature is perfectly different from Wordsworth's.   He has
neither the unbroken peace nor the high contemplative joy
that no man could take from Wordsworth.   He reads his
own spirit of 'close-lipp'd patience' into the hills and
streams which for Wordsworth sang together in 'fulness of
bliss'—

> 'The solemn hills around us spread,
> This stream which falls incessantly,
> The strange-scrawl'd rocks, the lonely sky,
> If I might lend their life a voice,
> Seem to bear rather than rejoice.
> And even could the intemperate prayer
> Man iterates, while these forbear,
> For movement, for an ampler sphere,
> Pierce Fate's impenetrable ear;
> Not milder is the general lot
> Because our spirits have forgot,
> In action's dizzying eddy whirl'd,
> The something that infects the world.'—*Resignation*.

He escapes from this 'something'—which he elsewhere calls 'the infection of our mental strife,'—and the magic of nature gives him soothing but not rest; we feel it is a calm from which he may at any moment be plunged again in the feverish turmoil of 'new beginnings, disappointments new.' But while it lasts it is soothing of the purest and most healing kind, and Arnold brings the very soul of its quieting power into his verse. His debts to Wordsworth in poetic description of nature have been freely acknowledged; but in spite of his own tribute few, if any, seem to have noticed the influence upon this part of his work of De Senancour, the author of *Obermann*. Yet the tone of his lovely descriptive lines seems often more closely akin to De Senancour than to Wordsworth. Take the opening of *Empedocles on Etna*—

> 'O Pan,
> How gracious is the mountain at this hour!
> A thousand times have I been here alone,
> Or with the revellers from the mountain-towns,
> But never on so fair a morn;—the sun
> Is shining on the brilliant mountain-crests,
> And on the highest pines; but farther down,
> Here in the valley is the shade; the sward

> Is dark, and on the stream the mist still hangs ;
> One sees óne's footprints crush'd in the wet grass,
> One's breath curls in the air ; and on these pines
> That climb from the stream's edge, the long grey tufts,
> Which the goats love, are jewell'd thick with dew.
>
>   *   *   *   *   *
>
> What mortal could be sick or sorry here?'

That is very unlike the tone of Wordsworth on a mountain.
Take the sunrise in the first book of *The Excursion*—

>   ' When, from the naked top
> Of some bold headland, he beheld the sun
> Rise up and bathe the world in light !　He looked—
> Ocean and earth, the solid frame of earth
> And ocean's liquid mass, in gladness lay
> Beneath him ;—Far and wide the clouds were touched,
> And in their silent faces he could read
> Unutterable love.
>
>   ' In such high hour
> Of visitation from the living God,
> Thought was not ; in enjoyment it expired.
> No thanks he breathed, he proffered no request ;
> Rapt into still communion that transcends
> The imperfect offices of prayer and praise,
> His mind was a thanksgiving to the power
> That made him ; it was blessedness and love !'

Or take the lighter *First Ascent of Helvellyn,*—

>   ' For the power of hills is on thee,
>   As was witnessed through thine eye
>   Then, when old Helvellyn won thee
>   To confess their majesty !'

But, making due allowance for the difference between poetry
and prose, it is not at all unlike passages in the letters of
'Obermann.'　And the two poems on *Obermann* breathe
the spirit of De Senancour's feeling for nature at least as
faithfully as in the pages of *Obermann,*

> 'the mountain-murmur swells
> Of many a dark-bough'd pine.'

But whatever affinities Arnold may have, his manner is after all distinctly his own. Coleridge, speaking of nature described by genius, says, ' Like a green field reflected in a perfectly calm and transparent lake, the image is distinguished from the reality only by its greater softness and lustre. Like the moisture or the polish on a pebble, genius neither distorts nor false-colours its objects ; but on the contrary brings out many a vein and many a tint, which escape the eye of common observation, thus raising to the rank of gems what had been often kicked away by the hurrying foot of the traveller on the dusty high-road of custom.' [1] Both parts of the comparison are singularly applicable to Arnold's pictures of Nature, which have just the stillness and brightness needful to a perfect reflection, and combine with that the lustrous polish due to his deliberate, scholarlike workmanship. Here is a single stanza from *Thyrsis* delineating one of the much-loved pathways near Oxford.

> ' Runs it not here, the track by Childsworth Farm,
>   Past the high wood, to where the elm tree crowns
>   The hill behind whose ridge the sunset flames ?
>   The signal-elm, that looks on Ilsley Downs,
>   The vale, the three lone weirs, the youthful Thames ?—
>   This winter-eve is warm,
>   Humid the air ! leafless, yet soft as spring,
>   The tender purple spray on copse and briers !
>   And that sweet city with her dreaming spires,
>   She needs not June for beauty's heightening.'

How peaceful and clear and gentle it all is ! How delicately the melancholy pleasure of revisiting a once familiar spot is

[1] *Literaria Biographia*, vol. ii.

implied in the questioning tone, the description as much from memory as sight. And with what tender grace each point is noted ; the 'signal elm,' 'lone weirs,' the 'youthful Thames,' the rich winter colouring on copse and briers, so often passed unseen even by dwellers in the country, who, if they were asked, would call the leafless twigs and hedges black. Especially are we carried out of the region of dull prose and commonplace by the one exquisite line and epithet—

> 'That sweet city with her dreaming spires.'

Many another equally beautiful retreat from dust and din is to be found in Arnold's poetry. Here is the dying away of summer daylight among the high Alps.

> 'How often where the slopes are green
>   On Jaman, hast thou sate
> By some high châlet-door, and seen
>   The summer-day grow late ;
>
> 'And darkness steal o'er the wet grass
>   With the pale crocus starr'd,
> And reach that glimmering sheet of glass
>   Beneath the piny sward,
>
> 'Lake Leman's waters, far below !
>   And watch'd the rosy light
> Fade from the distant peaks of snow ;
>   And on the air of night
>
> 'Heard accents of the eternal tongue
>   Through the pine branches play—
> Listen'd, and felt thyself grow young !
>   Listen'd and wept.'—*Obermann.*

How closely and lovingly he has observed, how happily the spirit of what he sees has entered into him, is evidenced by frequent passing phrases—the 'wet, bird-haunted English lawn,' 'roses that down the alleys shine afar,' 'Sweet-William with his homely cottage-smell.'

Through his fine sense for the expressiveness of words and idioms, Arnold's verse lays his readers under a spell whose secret is the power of strength in simplicity.   One stanza from *Obermann* is enough to illustrate—

> ' A fever in these pages burns
>   Beneath the calm they feign ;
> A wounded human spirit turns
>   Here, on its bed of pain.'

Not a single vehement word ; but a whole paragraph of vehemence would leave a weaker impression of spiritual agony.   There is nothing in the least childlike or homely in simplicity of this kind ; nor is it like Wordsworth's simplicity, even in his later, more artistic work.   It is like Newman's use of words in prose, the outcome of a finely disciplined taste, able to use in a modern language the severely pure style learnt in classical schools.

It will be noticed how few love-poems Arnold has written ; on the other hand his work is peculiarly rich in the number and beauty of his elegiac poems.   Commemoration of fore-runners and friends who for any reason have stood apart from the 'world' he so unsparingly condemns, gives the best scope for his gravity and sweetness, for the contrast he draws between the world's life and life which is not of it, for his sense of the consoling power of Nature.   Whether he commemorates men or creeds, or even his domestic pets, these poems, never stormily nor bitterly sorrowful, are full of pure deep feeling, gentle melancholy, yearning regret, often quite as touching as more demonstrative grief.   And he has the gift of gifts for an elegiac poet of leaving both persons and places the dearer to us for his words.   Even spots sacred to

Wordsworth seem the more lovable for Arnold's reverie over them.

> 'The spots which recall him survive,
> For he lent a new life to these hills.
> The Pillar still broods o'er the fields
> Which border Ennerdale Lake,
> And Egremont sleeps by the sea.
> The gleam of the evening star
> Twinkles on Grasmere no more,
> But ruined and solemn and grey
> The sheepfold of Michael survives ;
> And, far to the south, the heath
> Still blows in the Quantock coombs
> By the favourite waters of Ruth.'
>
> *The Youth of Nature.*

The twin poems *The Scholar Gypsy* and *Thyrsis* are among the most beautiful of these ; the latter, a memorial to A. H. Clough, has borne comparison with *Lycidas* and *Adonais.* Arnold rarely uses an elaborate metre, but he does so both in these two and in *Westminster Abbey,* and perhaps the one stanza already quoted from *Thyrsis* is enough to show how admirably such a metre suits his work.

Memorial Verses celebrate, with keen insight, Byron's stormy passion and daring, Goethe's dissecting skill, Wordsworth's 'healing power.' *Heine's Grave,* besides its estimate of the dead poet, contains in a mournfully grand image, Arnold's judgment of modern England,—

> 'For her sons,
> Long since, deep in our hearts,
> Echo the blame of her foes.
> We, too, sigh that she flags ;
> We, too, say that she now—
> Scarce comprehending the voice
> Of her greatest, golden-mouth'd sons
> Of a former age any more—

Stupidly travels her round
Of mechanic business, and lets
Slow die out of her life
Glory and genius and joy.

    *   *   *

'Yes, we arraign her! but she,
The weary Titan, with deaf
Ears, and labour-dimm'd eyes,
Regarding neither to right
Nor left, goes passively by,
Staggering on to her goal ;
Bearing on shoulders immense,
Atlanteän, the load,
Wellnigh not to be borne,
Of the too vast orb of her fate.'

Rugby Chapel, the tribute of a gifted son to a noble father, honouring to both, is probably better known than any other poem of Arnold's except *The Forsaken Merman*. *A Southern Night* was written in memory of his brother; *Haworth Churchyard* in honour of the Brontë sisters, and incidentally of Harriet Martineau. Many years later, when Arnold was once more induced to break the silence which, as a poet, he had kept so long, it was to take up the elegiac strain again in three final poems— *Westminster Abbey*, *Geist's Grave*, *Poor Matthias*—whose chastened beauty shows that his hand had lost none of its cunning. Of these, one must give the name of the dachshound Geist, his 'little friend,' even tenderer associations in literature than belong to Cowper's 'Beau,' or Mrs. Browning's 'Flush'; and all birds should be dearer for the sake of this poet's still tinier canary-friend Matthias. It would be hard to find poems more genuinely and exquisitely pathetic than these two. Arnold lays as sure a finger on the nature of his favourites as on that of friends or brother poets. Who does not instantly endorse his reading of 'Atossa,' the magnificent Persian?

> '—Cruel, but composed and bland,
> Dumb, inscrutable and grand,
> So Tiberius might have sat,
> Had Tiberius been a cat.'

And yet how touchingly he realises the baffling impossibility of *real* communion between natures so widely sundered as those of men and birds—

> 'What they want we cannot guess,
> Fail to track their deep distress,'

—nay, even between separate human souls.

> 'What you feel escapes our ken—
> Know we more our fellow men?
> Human suffering at our side,
> Ah, like yours is undescried!
> Human longings, human fears,
> Miss our eyes and miss our ears.
> Little helping, wounding much,
> Dull of heart, and hard of touch,
> Brother man's despairing sign
> Who may trust us to divine?
> Who assure us, sundering powers
> Stand not 'twixt his soul and ours?'—*Poor Matthias.*

It is the same feeling that dictated the wonderful line which, in an earlier poem, concludes his comparison of human souls to islands having between their shores—

> 'The unplumb'd, salt, estranging sea.'

Lastly there are the three finest of all these poems— *Stanzas from the Grande Chartreuse,* and the two on Obermann, of which the first has already been quoted more than once. In these Arnold's intellectual position is made

especially clear; and here too we have his lingering sympathy with a faith he feels himself too clear-sighted to
accept. He describes the rugged approaches to the famous
Carthusian monastery, the rigid seclusion, the austere life,
the penitential observances of the brotherhood, and then
suddenly asks himself what right has *he* to be there?

> 'For rigorous teachers seized my youth,
>   And purged its faith, and trimm'd its fire,
> Show'd me the high, white star of Truth,
>   There bade me gaze, and there aspire.
> Even now their whispers pierce the gloom :
> *What dost thou in this living tomb ?*
>
> 'Forgive me, masters of the mind !
>   At whose behest I long ago
> So much unlearnt, so much resign'd—
>   I come not here to be your foe !
> I seek these anchorites, not in ruth,
> To curse and to deny your truth ;
>
> 'Not as their friend, or child, I speak !
>   But as, on some far northern strand,
> Thinking of his own Gods, a Greek
>   In pity and mournful awe might stand
> Before some fallen Runic stone—
> For both were faiths, and both are gone.
>
> 'Wandering between two worlds, one dead,
>   The other powerless to be born,
> With nowhere yet to lay my head,
>   Like these, on earth I wait forlorn.
> Their faith, my tears, the world deride
> I come to shed them at their side.'

The second poem on Obermann—*Obermann Once More*
—has lost even the hopeless hope of the first. Its magnificent pictures of Roman and Eastern civilization, the
decay of the one and stagnation of the other, lead up to a
requiem over the tomb of Christianity—

156 VICTORIAN POETS.

'Now he is dead!   Far hence he lies
    In the lorn Syrian town;
And on his grave, with shining eyes,
    The Syrian stars look down.

*   *   *   *

' *Unduped of fancy, henceforth man
    Must labour!—must resign
His all too human creeds, and scan*
    Simply the way divine!'

From the sore pain and desolation that follow, the poem,
after vague hints at a new order as yet too imperfectly
beheld to give much consolation, subsides into the only
assuagement the poet has to command—a soothing con-
templation of Obermann's noble mountain haunts.

'Soft darkness on the turf did lie.
    Solemn, o'er hut and wood,
In the yet star-sown nightly sky,
    The peak of Jaman stood.

*   *   *   *

' And glorious there, without a sound,
    Across the glimmering lake,
High in the Valais-depth profound,
    I saw the morning break.'

'No one,' says Mr. Hutton, summing up what Arnold's
poetry has done for this generation, 'no one has expressed
more powerfully and poetically its spiritual weaknesses, its
craving for a passion that it cannot feel, its admiration for
a self-mastery that it cannot achieve, its desire for a creed
that it fails to accept, its sympathy with a faith that it will
not share, its aspiration for a peace that it does not know.'

V

DANTE GABRIEL ROSSETTI.
WILLIAM MORRIS.
ALGERNON CHARLES SWINBURNE.

' ——He holds that, paint a body well,
You paint a soul by implication, like
The grand first Master.'

Aurora Leigh.

' I HATE long poems,' wrote Rossetti, and acted up to his
word. But the moderate-sized volume of his songs, ballads
and sonnets adds an entirely new and very remarkable
element to the already rich stores of Victorian poetry.

Born in London in 1828, the eldest son of an Italian
father and a mother whose parentage was half Italian and
half English, Rossetti's artistic character was naturally
moulded under very different influences from that of most
English poets. In early youth he showed signs of the
double genius for painting and literature which afterwards
distinguished him as one of the very few men who have
reached eminence in both. At nineteen or twenty he was
a leader in the little band of enthusiastic young artists who,
revolting from the then received and conventional methods
of picture-making, resolved to trust their own hearts and
eyes, and went back to early Italian masters for sincerity
and simplicity of style. In Mr. Ruskin's phrase, their aim

was to 'paint nature as it is around them, with the help
of modern science.' Half jokingly they were dubbed the
'Pre-Raphaelite Brotherhood,'—a name that is now perhaps
more familiar than well understood.

After a ten years' friendship, Rossetti married in 1860
Miss Eleanor Siddons, the daughter of a Sheffield optician,
whose beauty and artistic susceptibilities were his joy and
pride. Within two years the sudden death of this idolised
wife from an overdose of laudanum drove Rossetti into a
life of seclusion. He buried himself in a sombrely picturesque old house in Cheyne Walk, attracted chiefly by a
garden large enough to allow him to take exercise in private;
and although his painting and literary work were pursued
as before, he never resumed his old habits of social inter-
course, keeping himself strictly to the society of a small
number of intimate friends. Twenty more years, chequered
with praise and blame, brightness and deep gloom, work,
weariness, and the solace of friendship, were his; and then,
his health of body and peace of mind alike shattered by the
use of narcotic drugs whose treacherous aid he had called
in to combat his misery of sleeplessness, he died in the
arms of his two devoted friends, Mr. Theodore Watts and
Mr. Hall Caine, on Easter Sunday, 1882.

Early as Rossetti's powers came to maturity, he was over
forty before he published a book of poems. Up to that
time only a few lyrics and sonnets had appeared now and
then in magazines, and some others were circulated to
some extent in manuscript; but the greater number, Rossetti,
in the first paroxysm of grief at his wife's death, had declared
to be hers and hers alone, and he had the manuscript book
in which they were written buried with her. For seven
years they lay in her grave; then the coffin was exhumed

and the poems recovered. When in 1870 his long-expected volume of *Poems* at last came out, it was received with an outburst of approving enthusiasm; but presently it drew down upon him, from the pen of a brother-poet, fierce charges of sensuality and debased moral feeling. Mr. Robert Buchanan, writing at first with an assumed signature, published in the *Contemporary Review* an article which he afterwards enlarged to a pamphlet, called *The Fleshly School of Poetry*, and thus originated a heated and miserable controversy which embittered Rossetti's already sorrowful life, and for a while incapacitated him altogether. There was, no doubt, real ground for Mr. Buchanan's protest against certain tendencies towards sensualism in English society and literature; but his attack on Rossetti was levelled against the wrong man, and executed in the wrong manner. Two years afterwards he owned that his first fiercely unsparing judgment was a misconception arising from over-hasty reading, and he dedicated his romance, *God and the Man*, to Rossetti with the words—

> 'Pure as thy purpose, blameless as thy song,
> Sweet as thy spirit, may this offering be;
> Forget the bitter blame that did thee wrong,
> And take the gift from me!'

After such a withdrawal, the whole unhappy episode might well be passed over in silence were it not that Rossetti's poetry has still to contend with a clinging reputation for sensuality, and even of aggressive irreligion, strong enough to deter some lovers of poetry from reading it.

Rossetti's real function as artist and poet is most clearly and sympathetically set forth in the luminous article upon him written by Mr. Watts in the *British Encyclopædia*, which describes the part he took in what Mr. Watts, discarding the hackneyed and never very lucid term, Romantic, prefers to call the 'Renascence of the Spirit of Wonder in Art and Poetry.' Just as the pre-Raphaelites, headed by Rossetti, broke away from lifeless imitations of classical models, and from eighteenth-century materialism, into new regions of delight and imagination in painting, so Rossetti, deeply imbued with Dante's idealism, and attracted by eerie medieval legends and English ballad-lore, developed in poetry the like sense of beauty, mystery, and awe.

The new order of poetry inaugurated by Cowper, not so much consciously, perhaps, as through sheer force of sincerity combined with the quick true insight of a nature so loving that not even the dogmas of Calvinism could harden, nor religious despair embitter it, culminated on the side of nature-worship in Wordsworth.

> ' He was a priest to us all
> Of the wonder and bloom of the world,
> Which we saw with his eyes, and were glad.'

Rossetti's worship of beauty takes up another line, and is directed to beauty as manifested in human form,—in woman hood. Of beauty in 'meadow, grove, and stream' he took, for the most part, little heed; but he is as one haunted by a special type of womanly beauty, which he dwells upon again and again with a warmth of description foreign to English reserve, and apt to mislead hasty readers as to his full purpose. But looking a little longer we see that the object of his thoughts is no mere bodily beauty, but bodily beauty 'ennobled by the concurrence of the soul at all times,'—beauty

> ' Whose speech Truth knows not from her thought
> Nor Love her body from her soul.'—*Love-Lily.*

Love is for him a mystical passion; beauty the symbolic
expression of hidden, perhaps incommunicable spiritual
meanings—

> 'Shall birth and death and all dark names that be
> As doors and windows bared to some loud sea,
>   Lash deaf mine ears and blind my eyes with spray ;
>   And shall my sense pierce love,—the last relay
> And ultimate outpost of eternity ?'—*House of Life*, xxxiv.

And again,

> 'Lady, I fain would tell how evermore
> Thy soul I know not from thy body, nor,
> Thee from myself, neither our love from God.'
> *House of Life*, v.

And again,

> 'The shadowed eyes remember and foresee,
> Her face is made her shrine.'—*House of Life*, x.

Rossetti does not reiterate sentiments of this kind so often
as he might if he regarded himself as in any way charged
with a message ; but his poetry is conceived in the spirit of
them.   And further, he depicts the love generated by
beauty as touching, at its highest, an ideal in some degree
resembling Dante's, the love of one whose glance is
regeneration, whose worship lifts the heart to heaven,
where alone the Blessed Damozel can be approached.
There *is* a love also to destruction ; and although Rossetti
implicitly declares it to be no part of his object to
'strengthen God among men'—for 'when at any time
hath He cried unto thee, saying, "My son, lend me thy
shoulder, for I fall"?' [1]—yet it dawns upon us by degrees
that Mr. Hall Caine has shown the truest discernment of the
spirit of his poetry when he says, 'the topmost thing in him

[1] Rossetti's prose dream, *Hand and Soul*.

was indeed the love of beauty, but the deepest thing was the love of uncomely right.'

Touching religion, Rossetti is neither prophet nor priest nor saint nor assailant; he is simply not in the least concerned with religious struggles or searchings of heart. Without being a Catholic, his attitude in such matters is not unlike the unquestioning acquiescence of Catholicism. He returns in spirit to the childlike devoutness of early Italian painters, seeking for his artistic work an inspiration like theirs, though unfettered by asceticism, and guided by better scientific knowledge.

> ' Give honour unto Luke Evangelist ;
>   For he it was (the aged legends say)
>   Who first taught Art to fold her hands and pray.
> Scarcely at once she dared to rend the mist
> Of devious symbols : but soon having wist
>   How sky-breadth and field-silence and this day
>   Are symbols also in some deeper way,
> She looked through these to God and was God's priest.

> ' And if past noon, her toil began to irk,
>   And she sought talismans, and turned in vain
>   To soulless self-reflections of man's skill,—
>   Yet now, in this the twilight, she may still
>   Kneel in the latter grass to pray again,
> Ere the night cometh and she may not work.'
>
>   *House of Life*, lxxiv.

In many ways Rossetti seems rather a spirit who has strayed among us out of medieval Italy than a latter-day English poet. He is almost untouched by modern ideas ; the number of poems in which he displays any care or knowledge of what nineteenth century Europe might be thinking or doing, could be counted on the fingers of one hand. He escapes from our moil and toil into a region where the throbbing pant of the steam-engine is never heard, and

responsibility for the universe is never felt; and he carries
no dust-mark with him.

It will be remembered how Wordsworth and Coleridge,
as young men, settled to divide a large field of poetry
between them, in which division it was to be Wordsworth's
share to lift the commonplace into poetry, while Coleridge
would prove how strongly men's feelings might be stirred by
the supernatural treated with such simple conviction as to
produce a sense of reality. Hence the *Ancient Mariner*,
Christabel, *Kubla Khan*, casting their radiant spell. Keats,
too, just touched upon the secrets of 'faery-land forlorn' in
La Belle Dame Sans Merci and his lovely fragment, *The
Eve of St. Mark*. Where they visited, Rossetti seems to
draw native breath; he lives in an atmosphere of dream
and portent, witcheries and visions of angels; and his richly
pictorial style harmonizes with his subjects like a gorgeous
stained glass window emblazoned with medieval legend or
device.

In *The Blessed Damozel*, written at nineteen for the short-
lived and afterwards famous pre-Raphaelite organ the *Germ*,
Rossetti's power of rendering strange, unearthly beauty is at
once evident. The clear, bold imagery, the curious blending of religion and glorified love, the pure still depth of the
beautiful girl's meditations in heaven, the accessories toned
in harmony with her thoughts, leave a wonderful impression
of something indescribably pure and lovely, ethereal, evan-
escent, and yet human.

> 'Herseemed she scarce had been a day
>   One of God's choristers;
> The wonder was not yet quite gone
>   From that still look of hers;
> Albeit, to them she left, her day
>   Had counted as ten years.
>
>   *   *   *   *

' Around her lovers newly met
  'Mid deathless love's acclaims,
Spoke evermore among themselves
  Their heart-remembered names ;
And the souls mounting up to God
  Went by her like thin flames.

    *   *   *   *

' " When round his head the aureole clings,
  And he is clothed in white,
I'll take his hand and go with him
  To the deep wells of light ;
As unto a stream we will step down,
  And bathe there in God's sight." '

Like Coleridge's, such poetry as this tests the reader's own powers of imagination and poetic feeling ; its charm can no more be explained than the difference between red and green can be made clear to a colour-blind man. But happy are they who hold the passport of admission into these bright realms.

The Last Confession, Rossetti's only poem in blank verse, is a dramatic monologue in the manner of Browning, an out-pouring of highly-wrought passion not without its uncanny element in the ominous fate of the little glass-ware image of Love given by the patriot-speaker to the child he had kept in safety to his own constant peril. The sudden dread hurrying the frenzied lover into murder, the ever-withheld disclosure and the terror of it when made at last, are full of gloomy power ; the earlier transition of feeling in the speaker towards his charge is winningly beautiful.

' For now, being always with her, the first love
I had—the father's, brother's love—was chánged,
I think, in somewise ; like a holy thought
Which is a prayer before one knows of it.'

Among shorter poems, two exquisite love-songs are *The Stream's Secret* and *Love's Nocturn*—

> ' O water wandering past,—
>   Albeit to thee I speak this thing,
> O water, thou that wanderest, whispering,
>   Thou keep'st thy counsel to the last.
> What spell upon thy bosom should Love cast,
>   His message thence to wring ? '—*The Stream's Secret.*

In *The Woodspurge, Sunset Wings, Cloud Confines*, the mysteries of grief, hope, strife, speak from heart to heart.

> ' What of the heart of hate
>   That beats in thy breast, O Time ?—
>   Red strife from the furthest prime,
> And anguish of fierce debate ;
>   War that shatters her slain,
>   And peace that grinds them as grain,
>   And eyes fixed ever in vain
> On the pitiless eyes of Fate.'—*Cloud Confines.*

Most lovely of all, perhaps, is the musical, melancholy *Sea-Limits*—' Consider the sea's listless chime ' :—

> ' Listen alone beside the sea,
>   Listen alone among the woods ;
>   Those voices of twin solitudes
> Shall have one sound alike to thee :
>   Hark where the murmurs of thronged men
>   Surge and sink back and surge again,—
> Still the one voice of wave and tree.
>
> ' Gather a shell from the strown beach
>   And listen at its lips ; they sigh
>   The same desire and mystery,
> The echo of the whole sea's speech.
>   And all mankind is thus at heart
>   Not anything but what thou art :
> And Earth, Sea, Man, are all in each.

Rossetti was greatly attracted by ballad literature, and

a good deal of his most characteristic work is cast in the form of literary ballads, differing from the old, spontaneous, natural ballads in their complexity, condensed expression, and sometimes dramatic power. The refrains in particular, of which Rossetti makes large use, are often highly complex; occasionally the refrain is modified with every stanza, and keeps up a running commentary on the action. *Stratton Water* comes nearest to the old type without quite touching it. *Sister Helen* wields the supernatural in its terrifying aspects; the much ill-used term 'weird' is here exactly in place. As the deserted lady hears through the unsuspecting speech of her young brother, appeal after appeal to her mercy from the friends of her false lover, married three days since to another bride, and now dying in torment as the waxen effigy she has made wastes slowly over the fire; and as she holds on her course, though her heart breaks and her soul is lost by its success, we feel the grim force of relentless, cruel destiny, controlled by unearthly and evil powers. Hate fierce with the fierceness of transmuted love works its dark will through the dread ban of demoniacal witchcraft.

> ' " Oh the wind is sad in the iron chill,
>   Sister Helen,
>   And weary sad they look by the hill."
> " But he and I are sadder still,
>   Little brother ! "
>   (*O Mother, Mary Mother*
>   *Most sad of all, between Hell and Heaven !*)'

Rose Mary is another story of love misplaced and be-trayed, of supernatural aids invoked—but vainly; of guilt, expiation, death. We may contrast the moment of tragedy in a veritable ballad with this mother's dramatic cry on finding out the dead man's treachery to her daughter.

  ' " O what hills are yon, yon pleasant hills,
    That the sun shines sweetly on ? "
  " O yon are the hills of heaven," he said,
    " Where you will never won."

  ' " O what a mountain is yon," she said,
    " All so dreary with frost and snow ? "
  " O yon is the mountain of hell," he cried,
    ' Where you and I will go." '—*The Damon Lover*.

  ' She lifted the lock of gleaming hair
    And smote the lips and left it there.
  " Here's gold that Hell shall take for thy toll !
    Full well hath treason found its goal,
    O thou dead body and damnèd soul ! " '—*Rose Mary*.

The White Ship and *The King's Tragedy* are more ballad-
like.   The latter tells once again, with vivid freshness,
the story of the murder of the poet-King James I. of
Scotland, the narrator being Catherine Douglas, popularly
re-named Kate Barlass in memory of the part she took in
the King's defence.   The diction is simpler than is usual
with Rossetti, being carefully adapted to the time and
speaker.   The poem is steeped in supernaturalism, not
only as regards the imposing episodes of the phantom
woman's apparition, whose warnings against threatening
doom are powerless to turn the King aside, but also in
minor boding touches, as when, in the crisis of suspense
while the murderers search for the hidden King, the night
wind wails round the empty room, and the moonlit royal
shield in the window is suddenly left black.

    Critics are divided between the respective merits of these
ballads, or ballad-romances, with their pictorial qualities,
their movement and weird imagination, and of the sonnets
with their splendid diction, elaborate workmanship, condensed, emphatic style, and mystic idealism ; but on one

point they are not divided at all,—with one voice Rossetti is pronounced the greatest sonnet-writer of Victorian
times, not even excepting Mrs. Browning.   Rossetti loved
sonnet-writing, practised it from boyhood, and attained a
mastery in it undisputed among his contemporaries.   His
numerous isolated sonnets, especially those on pictures, well
deserve careful study ; but the first place is of course claimed
by his magnificent sonnet-sequence, *The House of Life*, a
series of a hundred and one sonnets devoted to love, grief,
change, fate, and other life-influences through which men
move.   No hasty reading is of the smallest use here ; even
with close attention it is often hard to follow the poet's
course of feeling from line to line or sonnet to sonnet, on
account of their 'arduous fulness' and highly condensed,
symbolic expression.   The rules of sonnet structure must
also be understood if they are to be fully enjoyed, and
a short analysis of structure may be more useful here than
a futile attempt to examine *The House of Life* at once
briefly and with justice.

A typical sonnet [1] consists of fourteen lines of five
dissyllabic feet (iambics as a rule), divided into two 'sys-
tems' composed of eight and six lines respectively.   The
first division, or 'octave,' is subdivided into two 'quatrains,'
divisions containing four lines each ; the second, or 'sestet,'
is also subdivided into two sets of three lines each, called
'tercets.'   The lines throughout must rhyme in a certain
fixed order.   The octave of a perfect sonnet has only two
rhymes, the first, fourth, fifth and eighth lines rhyming
together, and the second, third, sixth and seventh ; thus—

---

[1] The best exposition of the structure and history of sonnets is to be
found in Mr. Mark Pattison's introduction to his edition of Milton's
Sonnets.

a b b a   a b b a.

The sestet also has only two rhymes, following each other
thus—

c d c d c d.

There are, however, several recognized deviations from
this, the strictest form of the sonnet.   In English—poorer
in rhyming words than Italian, in which sonnets were first
written,—a third rhyme is often admitted in the sestet, the
rhymes being thus arranged—

c d e   c d e.

Sometimes, but less frequently, a third rhyme is introduced
in the octave, thus—

a b b a   a c c a.

Lines 1, 4, 5, 8 of the octave are regarded as its framework,
and in a true sonnet their rhyming is invariable.   Two
other essential rules are that the rhymes of the tercets must
not repeat nor resemble those of the quatrains, and their
order must never be the same as that of the quatrain
rhymes.

Double rhymes are as a rule inadmissible in a sonnet;
they overcharge it with sound in proportion to its length.
And the last two lines ought not to rhyme together, the
effect of this being to cause a break in the continuity of
sound, and to turn the two lines into a couplet separated
from the rest of the poem.   But on these points, and in the
number and arrangement of rhymes in the tercets, English
writers have allowed themselves more latitude than is given
by the recognized variations just described.   In doing so
their sonnets become more or less irregular; but it does
not follow that all sonnets not formally correct are therefore

failures. Their success can in each case be tried only on its own merits, and judged by a trained ear.

So much for the *form* of a sonnet. As regards the matter, the ideal sonnet is complete in itself; it is the expression of one, and only one, thought or feeling. Further, this thought or feeling is expressed in a manner answering to the formal divisions of the sonnet. It is opened in the first quatrain, enlarged upon in the second; then after a pause it is resumed in the first tercet, and is finally summed up in the last tercet. There ought to be no epigrammatic conclusion in the last two lines, for a corresponding reason to that which forbids a rhyming couplet at the close; for no fragment should be made so telling as to divide it from the rest, nor is any worked-up climax required; the flow of feeling in a sonnet, like the flow of sound, should be continuous and almost even throughout.

It has sometimes been objected that a kind of poem so artificial as this, bound by such stringent rules as to its composition and contents, must be opposed to the very nature of poetic inspiration, which demands absolute freedom to choose its own form—*make* its own form if needful. But poetry can give another pleasure besides that of a sense of freedom and spontaneity in the poet's utterance, the pleasure of fulfilled expectations when a known and prescribed law is beautifully obeyed. Just as the trained musician delights in the ordered 'movements' of a fine sonata, so in poetry the disciplined reader delights in the happy fulfilment of rules whose fitness has been proved and established by a long course of trials. There are many forms in which the poet can have all the freedom he desires; there is no other important form so strictly ruled as this,— for the *ballade* is not at present important, whatever it may become in the future. It is worth the reader's while to train himself to the reception of the sort of enjoyment this can give; it is worth the poet's while to minister to it. And indeed objections to the sonnet and its strictness do not come from the poets themselves; on the contrary, they have, as Mr. Pattison remarks, 'caught at the opportunity which the sonnet affords for distilling strong emotion into drops.'

Sonnets were first grafted on English poetry about 1540, and the first attempts show how difficult it was to naturalize them in a language so different from their native, flexible Italian. Then came Shakespeare's sonnets, varying widely from the strict type, for they consist of three quatrains closed with a rhyming couplet, and their rhymes are neither limited nor placed according to canon. It has been conjectured that Shakespeare followed the rules he knew, but did not know all. Milton, deeply versed in Italian poetry, recalled the English sonnet to the more beautiful and musical Italian form, and showed at the same time to what fresh and various uses it might be put. Before him the sonnet form had been employed only for love-poems, especially love-poems in which ingenuity of language was more certain than reality of feeling. In his hands the fitness of the sonnet to be made the vehicle of strong emotion, whatever its cause or subject, became no less manifest than the grandeur and stateliness of which it was capable. Only two of Milton's sonnets are on the same subject; no two in the same mood.

Once fairly established the sonnet has been stamped anew with the personal impress of almost every great English poet, receiving from one and another fresh associations of pathos, vigour, depth, majesty, serenity. Intensity of feeling generally tinged, sometimes saturated, with mystical imagination, extreme concentration, high-sounding music, richly elaborated diction, distinguish Rossetti's sonnets; and he has also, as Mr. Hall Caine points out, paid careful attention to the canon of comparatively recent development, that the thought or feeling should be presented in a twofold aspect. Every line, every word, one might almost say every syllable, is chosen with sedulous care for its effect; and the result is workmanship so equal that it is hard to select one example rather than another. Perhaps we cannot do better than end with the opening and final sonnets of *The House of Life*—

LOVE ENTHRONED.

'I marked all kindred Powers the heart finds fair ;—
　　Truth, with awed lips ; and Hope, with eyes upcast ;
　　And Fame, whose loud wings fan the ashen Past
To signal-fires, Oblivion's flight to scare ;
And Youth, with still some single golden hair
　　Unto his shoulder clinging, since the last
　　Embrace wherein two sweet arms held him fast ;
And Life, still wreathing flowers for Death to wear.

'Love's throne was not with these ; but far above
　　All passionate wind of welcome and farewell
He sat in breathless bowers they dream not of ;
　　Though Truth foreknow Love's heart, and Hope foretell,
　　And Fame be for Love's sake desirable,
And Youth be dear, and Life be sweet to Love.'

THE ONE HOPE.

'When vain desire at last and vain regret
　　Go hand in hand to death, and all is vain,
　　What shall assuage the unforgotten pain
And teach the unforgetful to forget ?
Shall Peace be still a sunk stream long unmet,—
　　Or may the soul at once in a green plain
　　Stoop through the spray of some sweet life-fountain
And cull the dew-drenched flowering amulet ?

'Ah! when the wan soul in that golden air
    Between the scriptured petals softly blown
Peers breathless for the gift of grace unknown,—
    Ah! let none other alien spell soe'er
    But only the one Hope's one name be there,—
Not less nor more, but even that word alone.'

———————

WITH Chaucer for his master, and the 'Renascence of
Wonder' for his school, William Morris has made himself
the prince of modern story-tellers.   He did not, however,
begin as a narrative poet, but published first, in 1858, a
volume of short romantic poems, *The Defence of Guenevere*,
and the dedication of this to Rossetti twelve years before
the latter's own poems appeared, was one of the first signs
to draw outside attention towards him.   Rossetti's influence
is very plainly perceptible in these poems; and there are
traces also of Browning's, chiefly in the monologue form in
which many of them are cast,—a form which in Morris's
hands produces a curious amount of obscurity, the very
last fault with which his later work could be charged.
Notwithstanding this the poems have a very attractive charm
of their own.   The volume came out before Tennyson's
Idylls of the King, and several of the poems have Arthurian
subjects, though much more slightly treated than by
Tennyson.   But the strongest and most characteristic poem
is the woeful *Haystack in the Floods*.   This is not a monologue, but tells in graphic narrative of the Lady Jehane's
comfortless flight with her lover from Paris, of their en-
counter with the foeman Godmar, whose company out-
numbers and overpowers Count Robert's, of the miserable
choice offered to the lady to live with the man she hates,
or be returned to Paris to undergo ordeal by fire or water,

of her dreamless sleep on the wretched heap of sopped hay,
and pitiful awakening—

> 'She
> Being waked at last, sigh'd quietly
> And strangely childlike came, and said:
> "I will not."'

And then follows the straining, foiled attempt of the pair
to exchange a last kiss, the horror of his death before her
eyes, the oversetting of her reason.

> 'She shook her head and gazed awhile
> At her cold hands with rueful smile,
> As though this thing had made her mad.
>
> This was the parting that they had
> Beside the haystack in the floods.'

Seven years later the long but fascinating story of *The
Life and Death of Jason* showed that Morris had found his
own special line, and already attained mastery in it; and
this was quickly followed by the great work on which his
fame must chiefly rest—*The Earthly Paradise.*

The plan of *The Earthly Paradise* is taken from Chaucer,
but developed with more completeness and symmetry.
The three different metres in which it is written are all
Chaucerian; but the modern poet differs from the elder in
having less dramatic power, and in carefully eschewing
contemporary affairs. He is, he tells us, 'the idle singer of
an empty day'—

> 'Dreamer of dreams, born out of my due time,
> Why should I try to set the crooked straight?'

And so he carries himself and his readers far back into
the days of ancient song and fable, and the lands of myth
and miracle—

> 'Telling a tale of times long passed away,
> When men might cross a kingdom in a day,
> And kings remembered they should one day die,
> And all folk dwelt in great simplicity.'

The *Prologue* describes how 'certain gentlemen and mariners of Norway, having considered all they had heard of the Earthly Paradise, set sail to find it,' and the adventurers, having after many years reached a distant western land, narrate the history of their travels to the strange people among whom they thenceforth dwell and are held in high honour. Twice a month, when solemn festival is held, a tale is related; and the poem contains the twenty-four tales that occupy one year, beginning in the spring-time. In the first half the subjects of the tales are alternately classical and medieval; before the work was finished Mr. Morris had come under the attraction of Icelandic literature, and in the later parts stories of Scandinavian origin are introduced, one of which, *The Lovers of Gudrun*, is the most powerful of any.

Morris does not invent either his forms or the groundwork of his tales; but taking the old verse or the old legend, he re-animates it, refines away what was coarse in its primitive structure, supplies deficiencies whether in motive or symmetry, breathes new vigour and sweetness into its life, and clothing all with delicate grace and beauty, produces a whole as original in workmanship as it is beautiful in effect.

Detailed analysis of these tales would be useless, even if their length did not put it out of the question. No one who has access to them can have the smallest difficulty in following their clear, smooth, beguiling narrative; as before said, they consistently avoid all stress of heart-searching topics; and the charm of their execution is exactly what analysis kills instead of demonstrating. It must be enough to say a word or two about some general characteristics.

The extreme ease of narrative and rhythm is one of these, producing a corresponding sense of restfulness in the reader's mind. At the same time monotony is escaped by variety of subject and changes in metre. Another lies in the delightfully fresh descriptions of nature, not given in great detail, but conspicuously faithful, and exhaling the sweet wholesome breath of the open air. 'Mr. Morris,' it has been said, 'is never so much at home as when he is out of doors.'[1] The lovely preludes to the different months are no unfair examples.

> 'Here then, O June, thy kindness will we take;
> And if indeed but pensive men we seem,
> What should we do? thou wouldst not have us wake
> From out the arms of this rare happy dream
> And wish to leave the murmur of the stream,
> The rustling boughs, the twitter of the birds,
> And all thy thousand peaceful happy words.'

The landscapes in *The Man born to be a King* are especially noteworthy; and here is another choice little picture from the dreamland *Story of Cupid and Psyche*—

> 'A lovely grassy valley could she see,
> That steep grey cliffs upon three sides did bound,
> And under these, a river sweeping round,
> With gleaming curves the valley did embrace,
> And seemed to make an island of that place;
> And all about were dotted leafy trees,
> The elm for shade, the linden for the bees,
> The noble oak, long ready for the steel
> That in that place it had no fear to feel;

---

[1] *Our Living Poets*, H. Buxton Forman.

> The pomegranate, the apple, and the pear,
> That fruit and flowers at once made shift to bear,
> Nor yet decayed therefore, and in them hung
> Bright birds that elsewhere sing not, but here sung
> As sweetly as the small brown nightingales
> Within the wooded, deep Laconian vales.'

Now and then a more imaginative touch occurs in the treatment both of landscape and of persons—

> ' And underneath his feet the moonlit sea
> Went shepherding his waves disorderly.'
> *Cupid and Psyche.*

> ' The shadow of a long-forgotten smile
> Her anxious face a moment did beguile.'—*Ibid.*

But as a rule the verse keeps on an even way of placid beauty, never sinking into prose nor rising to any great height of passion.

Before the *Earthly Paradise* was finished, Morris had begun the translations of Scandinavian sagas which, thanks to his ease and simple directness in narrative, read like original poems. They are, naturally, even less modern in tone and style than the *Paradise;* and indeed in securing the proper effect of remoteness, the use of archaic words and expressions has threatened to become a mannerism; but that is a small blemish in a large field of beauty. But since the saga-poems had their day, another change has taken place; Mr. Morris, as we know, has been unable to refrain himself any longer from efforts to alleviate

> ' The heavy trouble, the bewildering care
> That weighs us down who live and earn our bread.'
> *Apology—Earthly Paradise.*

His songs have become *Socialistic Chants,* and among its other responsibilities, modern civilisation, with its imperfect control of the forces called by itself into play, has to answer for having drawn, or rather dragged, aside this poet from his ministry of beauty and refreshment.

MR. SWINBURNE began his poetic career in high revolt against reigning principles in morals, religion, and politics; endowed with a boundless gift of utterance, and entrenched in a theory that poetry, being an art, was privileged to say what it pleased so long as the verses were good. The natural result was an immediate and sharp collision between himself and the many to whose moral or religious sense he gave grievous offence. The battle, bitter on both sides, was fought out on the ground of Morals *versus* Art; Swinburne's position might perhaps have been turned more effectively and not less truly with the contention that as the artistic ideal *must* include meaning as well as form, to emphasise and cover with a glory of noble language ugly facts or ideas essentially degraded, is to set up an ideal as false artistically as it may be hurtful ethically. However, without recanting anything, Mr. Swinburne's later works have been cleared of the elements which made his earlier poems offensive; and there the controversy may well rest.

Like Matthew Arnold, Swinburne quickly tried his hand at drama on the Greek model, and with much better success, for his wonderful lyrical drama, *Atalanta in Calydon*, has all the life and fire that *Merope* lacks. The rhymed choruses, in particular, are a triumph of splendid eloquence. The plot of *Atalanta* is simple; the principal incident being the boar-hunt, in which the terrible beast sent by Artemis upon Calydon (in anger at the king's neglect in having offered sacrifice to all the gods save her alone) is slain by Meleager, whose mother Althea, queen of Calydon, had, soon after his birth, seen a vision of the three Fates standing over him to prophesy of him, of whom the last had declared that he should live only so long as the brand then burning were unconsumed. Althea, therefore, had caught away the brand from the fire and laid it up in safety. But Meleager laid the spoils of the boar at the feet of Atalanta, the huntress, highly favoured of Artemis, and when his uncles disputed this disposal of the spoil, he turned upon them and slew them also. And Althea, hearing of the death of her brothers by the hand of her son, cast the brand upon the fire, so that Meleager wasted away and perished.

Every speech adds something to the movement or detail of the drama; the chorus keeps up its due commentary on the action; and Swinburne's own tendency to excess is kept in check by the severely restrained form of Greek tragedy. The animating motive of the whole play—the futility of resistance to the high gods—is chiefly developed by the chorus. After the exquisite introductory celebration of spring, the first considerable chorus, 'Before the beginning of years,' comes as a mournful piece of fatalism, almost subdued in tone. It tells how with weeping and laughter, loathing and love, the gods fashioned 'the holy spirit of man'—

> 'In his heart is a blind desire,
>   In his eyes foreknowledge of death;
> He weaves, and is clothed with derision;
>   Sows, and he shall not reap;
> His life is a watch or a vision
>   Between a sleep and a sleep.'

The next chorus, 'We have seen thee, O Love, thou art

fair; thou art goodly, O Love,'[1] occurs immediately after Althea's distressful warnings to her son against the attractions of Atalanta, have been answered in the speech that shows how, in spite of the exceeding tenderness and loyalty of his attitude towards her—

> 'For there is nothing terribler to men
> Than the sweet face of mothers, and the might',

—Meleager is nevertheless irresistibly impelled to thwart her wishes in this matter. Celebrating the glorious goddess of Love, it magnificently bewails the additional anguish brought through her means upon unhappy man.

> 'For bitter thou wast from thy birth,
>   Aphrodite, a mother of strife;
> For before thee some rest was on earth,
>   A little respite from tears,
>   A little pleasure of life.'

Was there not evil enough already on the sad earth for man—

> 'That thou must come after these,
> That thou must lay on him love?'

In the great central chorus, 'Who hath given man speech?' Swinburne includes a passionate arraignment of the ways of the Most High among men such as could hardly have come in reality from the lips of Greek polytheists. The chorus begins in bitter complaints against 'the gods,' but presently accusation narrows down its object to

> 'The supreme evil, God';

and the torrent of eloquent denunciation that follows seems evidently directed against Jehovah rather than Zeus.

---

[1] This chorus is contained in the volume of 'Selections' under the name of *Anadyomene*.

In this we have an anticipation of the passionate anti-theism to which in some of his later poems Swinburne gives utterance in his own person,—with, however, one essential difference in attitude. For the chorus in *Atalanta* denounces God believed in *as* God; but in *Songs before Sunrise* the poet speaks as one firmly convinced that the ideas of God-head and Christianity are purely figments of human fancy, and not only so, but that they are pernicious ideas, obstructive hindrances from the first to real progress. To most of us it will appear that his historic sense has signally failed him here; and he stands in marked contrast to Matthew Arnold, who, with an equal persuasion of the baseless origin of these 'all too human creeds,' can still write of men's religions—

> ' Which has not taught weak wills how much they can,
> Which has not fall'n on the dry heart like rain?
> Which has not cried to sunk, self-weary man:
>   *Thou must be born again!'—Progress.*

But the fact is so, and in any fair judgment of Swinburne, has to be taken into account. In virtue of it we cannot fail to see that his attitude of scornful derision in *Before a Crucifix* and the *Hymn of Man*, closely resembles that which is commonly tolerated in Elijah when he mocked the priests and worshippers of Baal.

> ' Thy slave that slept is awake; thy slave but slept for a span;
> Yea, man thy slave shall unmake thee, who made thee lord over man.
>   *   *   *   *   *   *   *
> Cry aloud till his godhead awaken; what doth he to sleep and to dream?
>   *   *   *   *   *   *   *
> By the spirit he ruled as his slave is he slain who was mighty to slay,
> And the stone that is sealed on his grave he shall raise not and not roll away.'—*Hymn of Man.*

There is also, however, a positive element in the *Songs*. Having repudiated theism altogether, Swinburne transfers many attributes of godhead, and frequently the name too, to 'the holy spirit of man.'

'Glory to Man in the highest! for Man is the master of things.'

On comparing passage with passage, this is the meaning that unmistakably emerges from poems that would appear, at first sight, to be pantheistic in bearing. For this 'God' a new day dawns—

'The sun re-arisen is his priest, and the heat thereof hallows his head.
His eyes take part in the morning ; his spirit outsounding the sea
Asks no more witness or warning from temple or tripod or tree.
  *   *   *   *   *   *
His soul to his soul is a law, and his mind is a light to his mind.
The seal of his knowledge is sure, the truth and his spirit are wed.'
Hymn of Man.

For him Swinburne now demands absolute enfranchisement, freedom like the freedom of Nature, liberty beside which ordinary republicanism shows as bondage. Triumphing in the political liberation of Italy and France, he sings as the herald of a brighter, more burning sunrise. Now mourning, as in *Mater Dolorosa*, over the wrongs liberty has suffered ; now invoking her like a lover his mistress, as in *The Oblation;* now flinging himself in a passion of hero-worship at the feet of Mazzini and others whose hands have upborne her ; now, as in *Mater Triumphalis*, exulting in her victory, the poet gives himself wholly to the cause of this 'dreadful mother' with heroic grandeur of self-abandonment.

'I am no courtier of thee sober-suited,
 Who loves a little for a little pay.
Me not thy winds and storms nor thrones disrooted
 Nor molten crowns nor thine own sins dismay.

  *   *   *   *

'I shall burn up before thee, pass and perish,
   As haze in sunrise on the red sea-line ;
But thou from dawn to sunsetting shalt cherish
   The thoughts that led and souls that lighted mine.
       *   *   *
'I am thy storm-thrush of the days that darken,
   Thy petrel in the foam that bears thy bark
To port through night and tempest ; if thou hearken,
   My voice is in the heaven before the lark.'

Mater Triumphalis.

After all, it is for the magnificent eloquence, the splendid
rush and rhythm of passages like this and countless others,
rather than for depth of thought or meaning, that we go to
the poetry of Swinburne.

A Song of Italy and *Songs before Sunrise* were followed
by new exercise of Swinburne's dramatic genius.   Another
fine play on classical lines, *Erechtheus*, came first ; then the
second and third plays in Elizabethan style of the famous
' Mary Stuart trilogy.'   The first of the trilogy, *Chastelard*,
as a presentation of the delirious and too often ignoble
passion which with Swinburne does duty for love, shares
with the first series of *Poems and Ballads* the worst objections to be brought against his early poems.   The second
stands out as the greatest of the three ; but neither Morris
nor Swinburne share Rossetti's objection to long poems,
and the physical proportions of *Bothwell* are, at first sight,
such as to strike alarm into the mind of even an intrepid
reader of dramas.   Whoever overcomes it will find the reward
in the play, of unbounded life and vigour, much interest in
characterisation, and Swinburne's unfailing music of sound.
Mary Stuart closes the tragic series with the crowning
tragedy of the Queen's own death.   All these plays give
evidence of the potent fascination that lay for Swinburne in
the riddle of her character and ill-starred career.

' Surely you were something better
    Than innocent !

' No maid that strays with steps unwary
    Through snares unseen,
But one to live and die for ; Mary,
    The Queen.'
                Adieux à Marie Stuart.

Tristram of Lyonesse exemplifies—at great length—
Swinburne's views of the way in which Arthurian narratives
ought to be treated. Among his remaining poems, two or
three subjects frequently recur, and are dwelt upon with
ever-fresh delight. One of these is the poet's devotion to
Victor Hugo, who has exercised so powerful an influence
over his work; another is his extreme love (Swinburne is
always in extremes) and admiration for little children.

' Where children are not, heaven is not, and heaven if they come not
    again shall be never :
But the face and the voice of a child are assurance of heaven and its
    promise for ever.'—*A Song of Welcome.*

Lastly there is the one object in Nature for which he really
cares, of which he never wearies—the sea; and perhaps no
single topic better illustrates the qualities of his verse than
this. His amazing command of language; his no less
wonderful mastery of metre, shown especially in his tro-
chaic and anapæstic measures ; his invention of new effects
in alliteration and other elements of sound; his musical
cadences ; his unchecked ease, sustained eloquence in expression, are all exerted to bring his hearers under a spell as
of the very sea itself, with all the sound and the glory of it,
the foam and fret, the salt spray and freshening breath,
the gladness and mystery and majesty, the storm and the
eternal peace. Yet in these poems we perceive his weakness as well as strength,—the slightness of actual meaning

that often underlies the splendour of sound, the curious
sense of monotony which so much unbroken harmony at
last produces.   Both suggest that the repeated comparisons
of Swinburne as a lyrist to Shelley, have been made with
more boldness than success.   To think of Shelley's lyrics
and monotony of any kind at the same moment requires
an effort which sufficiently marks out one difference between
the two poets ; and with all their beauty and impetuous
movement, Swinburne's measures have neither the ethereal
magic of Shelley's, nor his surpassing swiftness.   But no
comparison could either help or hinder our enjoyment of
such lines as these—

' The sea is awake, and the sound of the song of the joy of her waking
        is rolled
    From afar to the star that recedes, from anear to the wastes. of the
        wild wide shore.

        *   *   *   *   *   *   *

    Life holds not an hour that is better to live in ; the past is a tale that
        is told,
    The future a sun-flecked shadow, alive and asleep, with a blessing in
        store.
    As we give us again to the waters, the rapture of limbs that the
        waters enfold
    Is less than the rapture of spirit whereby, though the burden it quits
        were sore,
    Our souls and the bodies they wield at their will are absorbed in the
        life they adore—
    In the life that endures no burden, and bows not the forehead, and
        bends not the knee—
    In the life everlasting of earth and of heaven, in the laws that atone
        and agree,
    In the measureless music of things, in the fervour of forces that rest
        or that roam,
    That cross and return and reissue, as I after you and as you after me
    Strike out from the shore as the heart in us bids and beseeches,
        athirst for the foam.'—*In the Water*.

VI.

MINOR POETS.

'All round the room my silent servants wait,—
My friends in every season, bright and dim.
*   *   *   *
From the old world's divine and distant date,
From the sublimer few,
Down to the poet who but yester-eve
Sang sweet and made us grieve ! '

Barry Cornwall.

IT would be a most pleasant task to single out various groups and individuals from the great wealth of Victorian minor poetry, and look carefully into works at which present limits will allow nothing more than a glance.

No other poetess has reached Mrs. Browning's level of achievement, or anything like it; but there have been several whose poetry is nevertheless of no mean value. First she who, throughout the years of her short life on the wild Yorkshire moors, so dreary in winter, so divine in summer, might have been taken for their very Genius, incarnate for a while in human shape. Emily Brontë loved the moors with a passionate, personal love. She dreamed of them by night; she ranged over them by day; away from them she pined; in the bare, distant school-room her heart turns from the 'alien firelight' with sick longing for her moorland parsonage home; the midnight gale on the

bleak hill-side has its answer from her as from a votary.
The moors kept back no secret from her; their might and
gloom and glory and mystery breathe from every page of
hers, and above all their freedom, which to her dauntless,
untamable spirit was as the very breath of life.

> 'I'll walk where my own nature would be leading:
>   It vexes me to choose another guide:
> Where the gray flocks in ferny glades are feeding;
>   Where the wild wind blows on the mountain side.
>
> *Stanzas.*
>
> Oh dreadful is the check—intense the agony—
> When the ear begins to hear, and the eye begins to see;
> When the pulse begins to throb, and the brain to think again,
> The soul to feel the flesh, and the flesh to feel the chain.'
>
> *The Prisoner.*

But as a poet Emily Brontë had hardly thrown off the
trammels of conventional forms whose poverty of rhythm
disguised rather than expressed her will, before that last
terrible conflict came upon her, in which she wrestled
with Death as with a tangible and conquerable foe, '*would*
see, *would* hear, *would* breathe, *would* live up to, within,
well-nigh *beyond* the moment when death says to all
sense and all being—"Thus far, and no farther!"' Only
four or five poems are left worthy of her

> 'Whose soul
> Knew no fellow for might,
> Passion, vehemence, grief,
> Daring, since Byron died.'

There are the *Stanzas* and *The Prisoner* just quoted; there
is *The Old Stoic*, and the deathless passion of *Remembrance;*
and there are the last lines her hand ever wrote, her 'too-
bold dying song,' as Matthew Arnold calls it, the poem

of which Mr. Swinburne says truly that it is 'as utterly
disdainful of doctrine as of doubt.'

> 'No coward soul is mine,
> No trembler in the world's storm-troubled sphere :
>   I see Heaven's glories shine,
> And faith shines equal, arming me from fear.'

Very different in tone and strength is the tranquil,
melodious verse which has won for Jean Ingelow a rather
unaccountable degree of popularity. Her skill lies chiefly
in songs and in small, gracefully idyllic poems, where her
love for wild birds and flowers, especially the humble
ones, is conspicuous : when she moulds a little episode in
dramatic form, as in *Afternoon at a Parsonage*, or *Supper
at the Mill*, the incidental songs are much the best part of
it. One of her most successful efforts is the ballad-like
Winstanley, commemorating the first hero of the Eddystone
Rock Lighthouse ; another favourite is the tenderly mournful *Divided*, in motive somewhat resembling Clough's *Qua
cursum Ventus*, only here love takes the place of friendship,
and the two who in sport step down on opposite sides of
the tiny rivulet, see every inch added to the distance
between them by the course they cannot retrace. Hand in
hand they walk at first, but at last each moving speck is
lost to the other's sight across the broad river rolling
between them. But to my mind no other poem of Jean
Ingelow's comes up to *The High Tide on the Coast of
Lincolnshire*, telling in the homely sixteenth-century dialect
first of the peaceful rich green level pastures lying in the
golden sunset,—

> 'Where the reedy Lindis floweth ;
>   Floweth, floweth ;
> From the meads where melick groweth ;'

then of the alarm as the warning tune of Enderby came
floating over from the sweet-toned bells of Boston; of the
sudden disaster—

> 'So farre so fast the eygre drave,
>   The heart had hardly time to beat,
> Before a shallow seething wave
>   Sobbed in the grasses at oure feet:
> The feet had hardly time to flee
>   Before it brake against the knee,
> And all the world was in the sea ;'

—of the sorrowful bereavement so touchingly softened as it
falls from the aged lips of her who, without losing tenderness, is beyond the time for passionate grieving.

With less facility and melody, Christina Rossetti's poetry
has more thought, concentration, and imaginative genius.
Songs, sonnets, and short lyrics—many of them devotional
in tone—constitute its staple, with the exception of her best
known poem, *Goblin Market*.   They are very miscellaneous
in subject, and cannot readily be grouped ; each dream or
dirge or reverie has its own clear thought or emotion, and
one chiefly resembles another in its true poetic ring, and in
a prevailing sadness of tone such as to place her in our
minds among those who 'learn in suffering what they teach
in song.'   *To-day for me*, a lament for and with France in
1870, shares with *The Convent Threshold* and several
sonnets the distinction of having been singled out for
special approval by Dante Rossetti.   Among those
definitely religious in subject, *Despised and Rejected* is
one of the finest.

> ' "Friend, open to Me."—Who is this that calls ?
>   Nay, I am deaf as are my walls :
>   Cease crying, for I will not hear
>   Thy cry of hope or fear.

Others were dear,
Others forsook me ; what art thou indeed
That I should heed
Thy lamentable need ?
Hungry should feed,
Or stranger lodge thee here ? '

Goblin Market stands all by itself,—the happiest possible combination of serious fancy and mirthful earnest ; light and graceful on the surface with hidden depths below ; a tale out of elf-land, strange and bewitching to mortal ears.

Mrs. Hamilton King's principal volume of poetry, *The Disciples*, has perhaps come hardly, if at all, behind Mrs. Browning's and Swinburne's poems in quickening the sympathy of English hearts with the great mid-century struggle for the unity and freedom of Italy ; and in its consolations for the sick and weary touches chords which are never silenced by time. So well has this been recognised indeed, that one fragment, known as *The Sermon in the Hospital*, has been separately printed as a tiny pamphlet ; but it suffers by this treatment as the slow movement of a sonata suffers by detachment from its setting, though here the loss comes not through difference in style, but through the reader's inadequate knowledge of the preacher's character and the previous facts of his life.   They are such as to give peculiar force and meaning to his ministrations in the Hospital.   In the young priest of Bologna, Fra Ugo Bassi, who joined Garibaldi's army before the terrible disasters of 1849, and to whom the greater part of this volume is devoted, Mrs. Hamilton King delineates a character of singular beauty in its sweetness, elevation, and unchanged serenity, from his noviciate to the hour when, through protracted torture and in the face of certain death, he kept

the silence that screened Garibaldi's flight, so that it was
said of him at last—

> ' He savèd others from the perishing :
> Himself he did not save ! '

Few readers who remember the eager response of George
Eliot's sensitive soul to beauty in music, in pictured form,
in thought or word or deed, can wonder that she did not
rest without an endeavour to mould her own high thoughts
in the supreme form of poetry ; and perhaps the more
deeply they have felt the wonderful music and rhythm of
her prose, the more certain are they to be disappointed with
the heavy movement of her verse. She has indeed infused
some of her most characteristic views into her poems. The
sacredness of natural human ties ; the supremacy of duty
apart from the sanctions of God and immortality ; the post-
ponement of personal desires to the claims of a larger life,
are all enforced and illustrated in *The Spanish Gypsy* and
The Legend of Jubal. Responsibility is again driven home
in novel fashion in the quaint bit of dialogue between
Stradivarius the aged maker of Cremona violins, and Naldo
the *blasé* young painter—

> ' 'Tis God gives skill,
> But not without men's hands : He could not make
> Antonio Stradivari's violins
> Without Antonio.'

But hardly more than once does George Eliot's poetry attain
real freedom and singing power, and this occurs in her final
poem—an outburst of longing to share in the agnostic ideal
of ' life to come,' here conceived at its loftiest—

> ' O may I join the choir invisible
> Of those inmortal dead who live again

> In minds made better by their presence: live
> In pulses stirred to generosity,
> In deeds of daring rectitude, in scorn
> For miserable aims that end with self.
>
> *   *   *   *
>
> So shall I join the choir invisible
> Whose music is the gladness of the world.'

A marked feature of Victorian poetry is to be found in the number and beauty of its dialect poems, whether produced as occasional pieces, like the Laureate's *Northern Farmers*, or in the form of expression most natural to the singer, like many poems of the people, or written in dialect by deliberate preference of the poet. Among these last by far the most important place is held by William Barnes, 'the Dorsetshire poet,' for whose sake the loved county of his 'memory and mind-sight' should become as dear as the Wiltshire Downs for Jefferies'. Sprung from an old Dorsetshire family of yeoman rank, William Barnes worked himself up after his school-days through a small clerkship to the mastership of two successive schools. He further qualified himself for a degree at Cambridge, and for Holy Orders, which he took in 1847, at the age of forty-six. From 1862 the last twenty-four years of his quiet, fruitful life were spent as Rector of Winterbourne Came, between a country parson's active duties, and the pursuits of a scholar and poet. His mastery of languages was extraordinary; and he himself regarded his studies in philology as having at least as much value as his performances in poetry.

This was the life that supplied Barnes with the outward materials for the fusion his genius accomplished in poetry, the fusion—so rare as to be almost unique—of spontaneous, free, simple feelings proper to rustic folk with flawless poetic form. Country born and country bred, he remained so completely one in heart with the yeomen and peasants among whom he dwelt, that the only difference one can trace lies in the fact of utterance ; in him the peasants' dumbly-experienced thoughts and feelings become articulate. And then the other side of his twofold existence—his wide scholarship—comes in to replace the many faults of style which almost necessarily beset the spontaneous but uncultivated singer, by technique so perfect that it has been said of his eclogues and other pastorals, 'There has been no such art since Horace.' That his learning did not weaken the sympathetic bond between himself and his neighbours is indeed a matter of no small wonder. A country clergyman of highly intellectual habits commonly considers himself and is considered one of the most isolated of beings. A few years before William Barnes took Orders, a distinguished Cambridge graduate was presented to the Rectory of an obscure Midland village, where he was soon afterwards visited by a brother-clergyman, the hard-working and successful Vicar of a town parish. The visitor was shown both landscape and people ; looked, meditated, and took his way back to the town with the single remark at parting—' And the Lord shut him in ! '

However, Barnes did not feel himself imprisoned, and his cultivation only gave him the means of putting an outer form on his poems worthy of their humour and pathos, their sweetness and simple dignity. The Dorsetshire dialect, strange to other ears, though quite easy to master in print so far as understanding goes, has no doubt delayed such a wide recognition of their merits as may safely be looked for in time. One or two have undergone the indignity of being

printed by main force in common English—a kind of rough
treatment at least as fatal to these poems as it would be to,
say, *The Land o' the Leal ;* but literature takes care of herself in such a case, and rewards the aggressor by leaving
him with a lifeless body on his hands.   Well for us that it is
so, for there would be something peculiarly ungrateful in
such a defeat of the poet's favourite wish to preserve the
loved dialect of his native county.

The subjects of these pastoral lyrics are as various as the
range of character, circumstances, and landscape in rural
Dorset permits to one on whom no detail in the changing
days and years is thrown away.   Field and hedgerow and
stream, childhood and old age, are all dear to him, nor are
the stretches of middle life prosaic.   It is difficult to choose
from the numberless bits of picturesque description.   Here
is the breaking up of a summer storm—

> ' The drevèn scud that overcast
> The zummer sky is all a-past,
> An' softer aïr, a blowèn drough
> The quiv'rèn boughs, do sheäke the vew
> Last raïn drops off the leaves lik' dew ;
> *   *   *
> The sheädes that were a-lost below
> The stormy cloud ageän do show
> Their mockèn sheäpes below the light.'
>
> *The Sky A-Clearen.*

That notice of the returning *shadows* is as characteristic as
it is delicate.   Elsewhere he speaks of—

> The sheädeless darkness o' the night,

and he knows well the cold blue of shadows over snow—the
' vrosty sheädes,' he calls them—compared with the dusky,
chequered, summer shade of trees in full leaf.   In our days

of grass-cutting machines, perhaps we care more than ever
for the poetry of the old-fashioned hay-field—

> ' How soft do sheäke the zummer hedge—
> How soft do sway the zummer zedge—
> How bright be zummer skies and zun—
> How bright the zummer brook do run ;
> An' feäir the flow'rs do bloom, to feäde
> Behind the swayen mower's bleäde.'

Another of these hay-field pictures, *The Child an' the
Mowers*, is touched with indescribable tenderness. A little
child has died from sunstroke in the heat, and the sad,
simple narration ends—

> ' He died while the häy russled grey
>   On the staddle so leätely begun :
> Lik' the mown-grass a-dried by the day—
> Aye ! the zwath-flow'r's a-killed by the zun.'

It would be hard indeed to imagine a more touching image
for the little life so easily overpowered, than this of the
fragile meadow flowers laid dying in the swath of new-mown
grass.

Country manners and ways of thought are presented with
abounding humour and insight in *A Bit o' sly Coortèn*,
The 'Lotments, *The Common a-took in*, *Wayfearèn*, and
many another too long to quote in whole and spoilt by
mutilation. The blessed rest of Sunday to the labouring
man ' in the wold vo'k's time ' comes in for many a word,
and there must, one feels, have been a wonderfully good
understanding between these flocks of Arcady and the
shepherd who could write of them as he does. It would
be delightful to trace his handling of the various relation-
ships of family life, from ' Gramfer ' and ' Grammer ' down-

wards, to follow all through the ' Married Peäir's ' story whose *Love Walk* begins so enticingly—

> ' Come, Esther, teäke, vor wold time's seäke,
> Your hooded cloak that's on the pin,
> An' wrap up warm, an' teäke my eärm,
> You'll vind it better out than in.
> Come, Etty dear ; come out o' door,
> An' teäke a sweetheart's walk woonce mwore.'

In *The Wife A-Lost* we feel the depth of the one great sorrow of his own life ; *The Wold Wall* consecrates the first sorrowful days of bereavement—

> ' The wall is wold, my grief is new.'

The Hollow Woak breathes the softened regret of advanced old age for things gone by now, but once familiar.

> ' An' all do show the wold times' feäce
> Wi' new things in the wold things' pleäce.'

Others, like *The Love Child*, touch more subtly-blended and deeper feelings still. But I can only hope that these few fragments may be enough to tempt new readers to test for themselves what scant justice can be done here to their claims upon genuine lovers of genuine poetry.

The nautical language of *Fo'c'sl' Yarns* is less of an obstacle than provincial dialects to readers unfamiliar with it, and these songs sung ' to unlock the treasures of the Island heart' have gone straight home to many who care to listen for the

> ' Romance
> Of nature, traversing
> On viewless wing
> All parallels of sect,
> And race and dialect.'
>
> Prologue to *Fo'c'sl' Yarns.*

Years ago, when *Betsy Lee* appeared alone in a modest little volume, it came into the hands of a brilliant young scholar, no poet himself but full of love for poetry, who, after trying it on various friends, must needs risk his reputation with the venerable Rector of his parish (not only a poet but so beautiful a reader that to read aloud before him was in itself an ordeal) by proposing to read it to him. Half pityingly the Rector's family arranged the desired interview, and the young man, feeling, as he afterwards confessed, that it was the boldest thing he had ever done in his life, and forewarned not to take it too much to heart if the Rector fell asleep as he almost inevitably would, set off, and was received with a courtesy likely enough to turn out the precursor of a fit of abstraction if not of sleep. He began; and bit by bit the aged poet's attention instead of wandering became fixed, nay, riveted. Which of the two was most moved by the time the reading was over, it would be hard to say; but *Betsy Lee* proved then, as many a time since, 'fit to make a body cry.'

Another dialect poet of no mean order is the well-known Edwin Waugh, the Lancashire compositor of whom his county has good reason to be proud. His poems fill several volumes, and he, too, has treasures of humour and pathos, the quick eye and guiding voice to the hidden soul of poetry concealed in strange places. *Come Whoam to thi Childer an' Me* is a good example, with the wife's appealing details about the homely cheer ready and the loving hearts 'rayther hurt' with waiting so long for her man, and the unexpectedly satisfactory end—

> 'God bless thee, my lass; aw'll go whoam,
> An' aw'll kiss thee an' th' childer o reawnd
> Thae knows, 'at wheerever aw roam,
> Aw'm fain to get back to th' owd greawnd

> Aw can do wi' a crack o'er a glass ;
>   Aw can do wi' a bit ov a spree ;
> But aw've no gradely comfort, my lass,
>   Except wi' yon childer an' thee.'

Here again is the cheery and humorous last stanza of the love-story of a certain great strong athlete and his little village-born 'missus,'—

> 'Oh, th' kindest mates, this world within,
>   Mun sometimes meet wi' pain ;
> But, if this pair could life begin,
>   They'd buckle to again ;
> For, though he's hearty, blunt an' tough,
>   An' Matty sweet an' mild,
> For threescore year, through smooth an' rough,
>   Hoo led him like a child.'

And *The Dule's i' this Bonnet o' Mine* is the prettiest possible forecast of another love-story quite as promising. 'Jamie' has a happy prospect before him in his warm-hearted bride, so sweet and modest and humble; at once so careful of her maidenly dignity and yet so full of fun ; bent on acting up to her code of propriety, but dreadfully afraid of not looking her best.

Writing both in dialect and ordinary English there have been many other democratic poets since Ebenezer Elliott's days, of whose poems some give real pleasure to the lover of poetry, and some are perhaps of more permanent value to the student of social history. From Thomas Cooper (the Chartist author of *The Purgatory of Suicides*), Joseph Skipsey, Samuel Bamford, Laycock, James Cooper, Aaron Watson, and a small host of other north country poets, many stirring verses might be quoted.

At the other end of the social scale we have in equal

wealth a sort of poetry for which we have admirable descriptions, but no satisfactory name,—' Occasional Verse,'
distinguished less by subject than style, by light touch,
refinement, sparkle, brevity ; very often marked by the
display of a certain fine irony, and invariably demanding
perfect technical finish.   It is in this kind of verse that such
highly artificial forms as the *ballade* and *rondeau* have been
successfully adopted.   Foremost among many, Edmund
Gosse, Andrew Lang, and especially Austin Dobson—and
Austin Dobson especially when he is reproducing the finest
flavour of eighteenth-century manners—come into one's
mind ; and no less delightful are C. S. Calverly's delicately
polished jestings in verse, or the choice little poems of W.
Cory's *Ionica*.   But hardly one of these poems would not
be fatally spoilt by fragmentary quotation.

Closely allied to them in character, although too long to
be classed as ' Occasional Verse,' and claiming more serious
attention, is W. G. Courthope's *Paradise of Birds*, in form a
play, on the lines of Aristophanes, abounding in pointed
and piquant satire on current fashions in dress, cookery,
politics, literature, science.   In Mr. Ruskin's Lectures on
Birds (' Love's Meinie ') there is to be found a line-to-line
commentary on one of the principal choruses, the book
being, as he says, ' too thoughtful to be understood without
such notes as a good author will not write on his own work ;
partly because he has not time, and partly because he
always feels that if people won't look for his meaning, they
should not be told it.'   He also quotes the lamentable
bewailings of the souls of the French Cook and the Lady,
both in Purgatory, and each suffering appropriate penal
torments for their misdeeds worked in the flesh on their
furred and feathered fellow-creatures.   There still is—or

ought to be—too much of the sting of truth in these expositions of what women's dress and men's gluttony can exact, and perhaps I may add, too much pain in the thought of the senseless, destructive cruelty they involve, for these parts of the poem to be approached in an altogether light-hearted mood; but probably the account given by Maresnest, 'a philosopher of the " Development " persuasion,' of the Origin of Species from the ' philoprogenitive Sponge' would delight Professor Huxley himself as much as anybody. Even with our present high standard, we do not often get poetry so packed with allusive significance as Mr. Courthope's.

Various other poets refuse to be grouped; among them may be mentioned Charles Kingsley, whose beautiful and moving lyrics lift him to a higher place than *The Saint's Tragedy* or even *Andromeda;* Sir Edwin Arnold, with his intimate knowledge and sympathetically faithful rendering of Asiatic ideals; Lewis Morris, whose least ambitious poems are perhaps the most successful—*Songs of Two Worlds* rather than the *Ode of Life* or *Epic of Hades*, and among the *Songs, Street Children, The Organ Boy, Love in Death*, rather than *Evensong* or *The Wanderer ;* and— more remarkable than any of the three, though as yet far less known—James Thomson, author of our one poem of unrelieved despair, *The City of Dreadful Night.* In him power and gloom and beauty meet to portray anguish and desolation so profound that only a fellow-sufferer can fully comprehend it. Here and there he says, ' some weary wanderer'

> ' Will understand the speech, and feel a stir
> Of fellowship in all-disastrous fight ;'

" I suffer mute and lonely, yet another
  Uplifts his voice to let me know a brother
    Travels the same wild paths though out of sight."'

To the dwellers in this dark City, the Inferno itself is a refuge—forbidden ; for none can muster the needful entrance-fee of some hope however small.   The poem concludes with an enthronement of Dürer's ' Melencolia' ; rightful Queen of the sombre, terrible City is she, in whose expression dawns

> ' The sense that every struggle brings defeat
>   Because Fate holds no prize to crown success ;
> That all the oracles are dumb or cheat
>   Because they have no secret to express ;
> That none can pierce the vast black veil uncertain
> Because there is no light beyond the curtain ;
>   That all is vanity and nothingness.'
>   Canto xxi.

It is difficult to leave aside Scottish and Irish poetry, but some mention, however inadequate, must be made of one other class of poems which has received interesting additions since the pre-Victorian work of Keble,[1]—sacred song, and other poems of religious life.   Christina Rossetti's devotional pieces have been already alluded to ; Bishop Heber, Archbishop Trench, Dean Milman, C. C. Fraser-Tytler (Mrs. Edward Liddell), Faber, Bonar, have in their different ways contributed much that is of value; and Cardinal Newman's *Verses on Various Occasions*, touching the hidden life with true poetic feeling, would throw fresh light, if any were needed, on the devotion and humility of his pure and lofty spirit.

[1] The *Christian Year* was published in 1827.

'But Thou, dear Lord!
Whilst I traced out bright scenes which were to come,
Isaac's pure blessings, and a verdant home,
    Didst spare me and withhold Thy fearful word ;
Wiling me year by year, till I am found
A pilgrim pale with Paul's sad girdle bound.'
                                        Our Future.

Who is not reminded of George Herbert ?—

        ' Whereas my birth and spirit rather took
                The way that takes the town ;
        Thou didst betray me to a lingring book,
                And wrap me in a gown.'

Perhaps one of the most poetically beautiful passages in
Newman's poetry is the angel's closing song in his longest
poem, the mystical *Dream of Gerontius*—

        ' Softly and gently, dearly ransom'd soul,
            In my most loving arms I now enfold thee,
        And o'er the penal waters, as they roll,
            I poise thee, and I lower thee, and hold thee,

        And carefully I dip thee in the lake,
            And thou, without a sob or a resistance,
        Dost through the flood thy rapid passage take,
            Sinking deep, deeper, into the dim distance.
                *   *   *   *
        Farewell, but not for ever ! brother dear,
            Be brave and patient on thy bed of sorrow ;
        Swiftly shall pass thy night of trial here,
            And I will come and wake thee on the morrow.'

One would not call F. W. H. Myers a ' sacred poet,' but
in *Saint Paul* he has accomplished a noticeably fine religious
poem, in which boldness and fervour are fitly enshrined
in gravely musical language and a metre of singular dignity.
Some idea of the general style of the poem can be gained
from even one or two stanzas.   He compares the spread

of the new divine knowledge to the steady, gentle overflow
of Euphrates—

> ' Even with so soft a surge and an increasing,
>   Drunk of the sand and thwarted of the clod,
> Stilled and astir and checked and never-ceasing
>   Spreadeth the great wave of the grace of God ;
>
> Bears to the marishes and bitter places
>   Healing for hurt and for their poisons balm,
> Isle after isle in infinite embraces
>   Floods and enfolds and fringes with the palm.'

No complete exposition of doctrine is so much as attempted, and in some respects St. Paul's views are obviously
modified—conspicuously so as regards his attitude towards
women—but the poem as a whole absolutely thrills with his
passionate faith and love and loyalty to the death.

> ' Whoso has felt the Spirit of the Highest
>   Cannot confound nor doubt Him nor deny :
> Yea, with one voice, o world, tho' thou deniest,
>   Stand thou on that side, for on this am I.'

INDEX.

A Death in the Desert, 67
A Forgiveness, 61
A Lover's Quarrel, 59
A Musical Instrument, 109, 111, 120
A Song for Ragged Schools, 112
Abt Vogler, 49, 54
Amours de Voyage, 128
Andrea del Sarto, 56
An Epistle, 64
Any Wife to any Husband, 61
Apparent Failure, 50
Arnold, Dr., 122, 138
Arnold, E., 200
Arnold, Matthew, xiv, xix, 137—156 ; his training, 138 ; dramatic and narrative poetry, 138—142 ; lyrics, 142—151 ; agnosticism, 144 ; stoicism, 145 ; refuge in nature, 146 ; style, 147—151 ; elegiac poems, 151—156, 178, 181, 187
Art, 27, 55—57, 110, 118
Atalanta in Calydon, 178
Aurora Leigh, 116—120

Bagehot, W., 135
Ballades, 170, 199
Ballads, Mrs. Browning's, 108 ; Rossetti's, 166
Bamford, Samuel, 198
Barnes, William, 192—196
Betsy Lee, 197
Blessed Damozel, The, 161, 163

Books, vii, viii, xx.
Bothie of Tober-na-Vuolich, 125—128, 130
Brontë, Emily, 186—188
Brown, Dr. John, 43
Browning, E. B., xiii, 103—120 ; life, 103 ; effect on work, 104—108 ; classical poems, 109—111 ; poems on childhood etc., 111, 118 ; on death, 113 ; love-poems, 113—115 ; on Italy, 116 ; *Aurora Leigh*, 116—120
Browning, Robert, xi—xiii, xviii, 40—102 ; alleged obscurity, 40 ; style, 42, 68 ; human interest, 43 ; ideal of life, 44 ; doctrine of failure, 46—50 ; nature, 51—54 ; music and art, 54—57 ; love-poems, 57—62 ; philosophical and religious poems, 63—68 ; dramas, 68—83 ; *The Ring and the Book*, 83—102
Buchanan, R., 159
By the Fireside, 62

Calverly, C. S., 199
Carlyle, T., 124
Casa Guidi Windows, 116
Chaucer, 5, 173
Christabel, 108, 163
Christian Socialists, 21
Christmas Eve, 52, 67
City of Dreadful Night, The, 200
Cleon, 63

Clough, A. H., xiv, 121—137;
life, 122—124; character of
work, 124; poems on social and
religious topics, 125—128, 130—
137; Arnold's Memorial poem,
152, 188
Coleridge, S. T., 108, 149, 163,
164
Colombe's Birthday, 73—83
Cooper, Thomas, 198
Cory, W., 199
Courthope, W. G., 199
Cowper, 6, 113, 120, 123, 160
Cranford, 7
Cristina, 60
Cry of the Children, The, 112, 120.

Dante, 5, 160, 161
De Senancour, 147, 148
De Vere, Aubrey, 29
Dialect Poems, 19, 192—198
Dipsychus, 130—132
Dîs Alitur Visum, 59
Disciples, The, 190
Dobson, Austin, 199
Dream of Gerontius, 202
Dürer, A., 201

Earthly Paradise, The, 174
Easter Day, 48
Easter Day (Naples, 1849), 133
Eliot, George, 191
Elliott, Ebenezer, 198
Emerson, R. W., 73, 124, 136
Empedocles on Etna, 138
Epictetus, 142, 145
Esmond, 115

Fo'c'sl' Yarns, 196
Fra Lippo Lippi, 56
Fraser-Tytler, C. C., 201

Garibaldi, 129, 190
Gaskell, Mrs., 7
Germ, The, 163
Goblin Market, 189
Goethe, 138, 142
Gosse, E., 199

Green, Professor T. H., 26

Hallam, A. H., x, 29
Heine, 144
Herbert, George, 202
Hexameters, 129
Higher Pantheism, The, 29
Homer, 142
House of Life, The, 168
Hugo, Victor, 184
Hutton, R. H., 156

Idylls of the King, 31—39, 173
In Memoriam, 5, 12, 29—31
Ingelow, J., 188
Italy, 104, 116, 128, 182, 190

Jane Eyre, 117
Jefferies, Richard, 10, 192

Karshish, 64
Keats, 163
Keble, 201
King, Mrs. Hamilton, 190
Kingsley, C., 130, 200

Lady Geraldine's Courtship, 109
Lang, Andrew, 199
Laycock, 198
Longfellow, 129
Love and Duty, 28
Lowell, J. R., 4
Lucy Snowe (*Villette*), 117

Mariana, 1, 3
Master Hugues of Saxe-Gotha, 54
Maud, 5, 22
Maurice, F. D., 26
Mazzini, 116, 128, 129, 182
'Melencolia,' Dürer's, 201
Metre, 5, 6
Milman, 201
Milton, xvii, 6, 31, 171
Minor Poets, xx, 186—203
Morris, Lewis, 200
Morris, William, xv, 173—178;
romantic poems, 173; narratives,
174—176; ease of style, 176;

descriptions of nature, 176 ; sagas, 177 ; socialism, 177
Myers, F. W. H., 202

Newman, J. H., 122, 151, 201
Nightingale, Florence, 124

Obermann, 148, 150, 151, 154—156
Occasional Verse, 199
Old Pictures in Florence, 57, 77
Oxford, 122, 125, 149

Palace of Art, The, 27, 49
Paradise of Birds, The, 199
Pattison, Mark, 168, 171
Pippa Passes, 53, 68—73
Pre-Raphaelite Brotherhood, 158, 160, 163

Rabbi Ben Ezra, 45, 46, 51, 66
Respectability, 59
Ring and the Book, The, 83— 102
Rizpah, 20
Rossetti, Christina, 189, 201
Rossetti, D. G., xv, 157—172 ; birth and parentage, 157 ; marriage, 158 ; first poems, 158 ; controversy with Buchanan, 159 ; poetic character, 159—163 ; ballads, 166 ; sonnets, 168—172
Ruskin, J., 157, 199

St. Paul, 202
Saul, 65
Schiller, 110
Shakespeare, 40
Shelley, 6, 31, 185
Skipsey, Joseph, 198
Songs before Sunrise, 183
Sonnets from the Portuguese, 106, 114, 115, 120

Sonnets, structure of, 168—172
Sophocles, 142, 145
Statue and the Bust, The, 47
Swinburne, A. C., xvi, 178—185 ; expression, 178, 184 ; dramas, 178, 183 ; antitheism, 181 ; poems on liberty, 181—183 ; sea-poems, 184

Tennyson, Alfred, x, xviii, 1—39 ; style, 4 ; knowledge of nature, 7 —12 ; idylls, 12—17 ; dramatic work, 18—21 ; social ideals, 21— 25; moral and religious problems, 26—31 ; Arthurian poems, 31— 39
Thackeray, 115, 133
The Worst of It, 61
Thomson, James, 200
Thring, E., 46
To Flush, 104
Too Late, 60
Trench, 201
Two Voices, The, 9, 27

Ulysses, 18

Victorian Drama, 69
Vision of Sin, The, 28

Watson, Aaron, 198
Watts, Theodore, article on Rossetti, 159
Waugh, Edwin, 197
Women's work, 119
Wordsworth, xviii, 6, 7, 11, 40, 138, 146, 148, 151, 152, 160, 163

Youth and Art, 59

THE END.